I0544974

Reflections From the
Write Stuff:
An Anthology

Reflections From the Write Stuff:

An Anthology

M. A. Estevis and Steven Ramírez, Eds.

Reflections From the Write Stuff:

An Anthology

Copyright © 2018 by members of the Write Stuff

All rights reserved, including the right of reproduction in whole or in part in any form, except for authorized reviews. Names used in this book are absolutely fictitious, except by prior agreement by named. Any inadvertent errors in permission or attribution will be corrected in the subsequent printing.

ISBN 978-1-7328280-0-1

Omni-Media Publishing
Edinburg, Texas

CONTENTS

(Contents continued)

(Contents continued)

*I*NTRODUCTION

What would make twelve people decide to publish an anthology together? Perhaps to make lots of money or to garner great fame? Probably not, as that is highly unlikely. Maybe the answer is because they have nothing else to do, or because writing is an easy task. That response is absolutely wrong. To answer this question, perhaps it would help to take a look at this group of individuals.

The Write Stuff writers' group was formed on September 17, 2014, at the Dustin Michael Sekula Memorial Library in Edinburg, Texas. Over the past four years, members have come and gone; however, a small core of writers has persevered with the biweekly tasks of submitting written work, critiquing the submissions of others, and rewriting and polishing their own endeavors.

The group is diverse in writing genres, with some preferring fiction, and others memoirs, essays, and poetry. Geographically they come to the group from South Texas, Ohio, Indiana, and as far away as Puerto Rico. They bring the wisdom of their ages, from thirty-one to eighty-seven, and the gifts of their chosen vocations: educators, salesmen, business men, chemical engineer, nurse, artist /musician, and even a published cartoonist. As reflected in this anthology, their education, life experiences, and wide-ranging writing skills are as varied as their interests.

So what would compel twelve people to publish an anthology together? The answer is simple – because they write stuff.

Maria Colvin-Lopez

Maria Colvin-Lopez is a first-time author who was born in San Juan, Puerto Rico, to an Irish father and a Spanish mother. From 1987 to 2012, she taught middle and high school students here in the Lower Rio Grande Valley of Texas.

For the last fifteen years of her teaching career, she spent researching the mystery of the R.M.S Titanic tragedy. She taught all she knew about this to her high school students. In the end, whenever she meets up with one of her ex-students, they tell her that they will never forget the six weeks of learning about the "whys and wherefores" of the mysteries of the Titanic.

In 2012, she retired and spent four years writing her own story about Titanic. In 2016, her book *Bonnie's Secret* was published. Currently she is working on the sequel *Nana's Legacy.*

Life and Death Reflections

My Silent Sibling

My brother last week turned 65 years old! My brother Roy has lived in a silent world all his life. What a roller coaster ride we have had with Roy.

He was born in 1950, when the medical world didn't know very much about mental retardation. When he was born, the doctors said he needed an operation to relieve the pressure on his brain but the operation had a 50-50 chance of success, so my father said "no" he didn't want to lose his son on the operating table and that we would take the chance of his life being limited. Dad said we had enough love to sustain him.

At the age of five, my brother learned how to walk but it was short lived when he fell and broke his leg. He broke it a second time when he was 10, and when it healed it was crooked, so from that moment on he was confined to a wheelchair.

Mother took full care of him until she couldn't lift him any longer at the age of 14. He was then sent to a home where he had round-the-clock care.

Our Christmas's were encircled around him because we wanted to see the joy written on his face when he opened his gifts of mostly cars and trucks. His birthday cake always had a car on it.

I remember one Christmas my younger brother Jerry received a small hot rod car he could ride in and Roy thought it was for him. Surprisingly, Jerry said, "Put him in the car."

Upon doing that, Roy started making the noise of a car's engine, "Vroom, vroom."

We couldn't get him out of that car for a long time, in fact, he took a nap in the car, he ate his supper in the car, and when he finally was so exhausted, father lifted him up and laid him in his bed. Roy had the most angelic smile on his face.

We, his siblings, had to protect him at all cost. When Mom and Dad decided he needed more help than what the family could give him, our hearts were broken because we could only go and see him once a week. In the winter time, it was even less because the Michigan roads were dangerous to drive on.

As time went by, we saw him grow less and less vocal, yet, he did make some sounds; in fact, he learned two words: Momma and hurt. Do you see the irony in these words?

Back in 1971, my mother called me to tell me that they had to move Roy one more time. He was 21 years old and he found a way to play a game with the nurses and doctors. He could roll his wheelchair down the hallways very well. He was very observant of everything around him. The home had installed a new fire alarm system and they had a couple of drills to see how fast the nurses could evacuate the patients out of the building. The fire alarm was installed on one side of one of the glass doors.

Roy pulled the alarm and it automatically locked the door he was behind. The button to turn off the alarm and open the door was right next to the alarm. The nurses hollered at Roy to push the button but he thought it was a game, so he just laughed and clapped his hands. It took the staff about five minutes to convince him to push the button. He felt so good because he had showed them he did have the capability of learning something even though he was being naughty and disobeyed rules.

They called Mom and said she had to find another facility for him in which to live. I believe Roy lived in about five different homes before he was in the last two facilities. He was in Grandville's home 18 years and the one in Grand Rapids (the one he is in today) 17 years.

***

Now it is 2015 and I have lived in Texas for 40 years, so I haven't been able to visit Roy that often. The last 10 years I have come once a year to visit Roy and my 92 year old mother and my two brothers Ron and Jerry and my two sisters Carmen and Norma.

Do you know why this visit was more painful than last year? Well I am turning 70 this year and I don't know how many more years I'll be able to board an airplane to visit my family. I know I am being selfish! When I left my brother this year he started to sob. It broke my heart to say goodbye for yet another year.

He has lost 25 pounds since I saw him last year. My sister Carmen said his throat is closing up on him so he has difficulty swallowing his food. The doctor says he has only a few years left. When we are ill we can tell the doctor where it hurts, but my brother can't communicate this, he just whispers hurt over and over.

Well dear brother Roy, hold on, sister Maria is going to come and visit again real soon. Don't give up yet please!

Brother's New Beginning

Thank you Brother Roy for waiting for your Texas sister to come for her last goodbye; I have arrived with a heavy heart. I, plus sisters Carmen and Norma, came to look deep into your eyes to find that your waiting period was coming to an end. You gave each of us a beautiful gift – a small smile with the understanding that you knew your time here was coming to a close.

I'll never forget the phone call sister Carmen received the following day. "Please come back to the hospital, Roy is slipping fast."

We arrived in record time and rushed to your side. You were gasping for air and we thought that you were pleading with the good Lord for more time.

Our brother Ron was at your right ear and our sister Carmen was at your left, softly whispering, "It's all right Roy – let go. God will carry you in His arms."

Over an hour and ten minutes later, your frail body and laborious breathing slowed until there was no more.

"Thank you, Lord, for bringing dear Roy to his heavenly home which he so dearly deserved, and thank you for ending his pain here on earth."

My hand was always wrapped around your hand so I gently pressed an angel stone between your fingers so that the angels would watch over you.

Now, dear Brother, you will be talking for the very first time, and I wonder what your first words will be. I know they won't be, "I'm hungry, or tired or cold." Maybe, they will be, "Where is my father?"

Dear Brother, you need to find the reserved table for the Colvins because you need to warm up a seat for our mom. Yes, dear brother, Mother will be joining you soon, for she is very grave with cancer. You must be ready to talk a long time with Mom because you have 65 years of catching up with the family.

Well, Brother Roy, you are not suffering anymore. You will have all the abilities you never had on this earth, and you have all eternity to use them.

Enjoy, dear Brother, for enjoyment will surround you now. I love you so much and miss you dearly. Rest in peace.

Reflections of my Mother

Mom, Grandma, Great-Grandma, Aunt, Sister, Cousin – all of these different titles she could fill in a way that no one else could. She was pure entertainment to the majority of us. She would host birthday parties, reunions, and for Christmas, she would dress up like Mrs. Claus; she was unstoppable.

Mom was born on April 14, 1923, in the capital of San Juan on the small island of Puerto Rico. She was born to Felipe Fagundo and Carmen Acosta, and she was the second child of five children.

As she grew up on the island, many started calling her "Fafin" because her middle name was Rafaela; this was her nickname. As she grew older, her mother taught her how to sew. As a family, they loved going to the beach in Cabo Rojo. Mom found out at an early age that she loved to draw and paint.

Later in high school, the big news event that filled the headlines was that World War II had begun in Europe. The war was going on when Mom met Dad in Puerto Rico. He was stationed there in San Juan. He had received a "Dear John" letter so he was really feeling lost. His buddies recommended for him to go out and mix with the native women of the island.

Mom attended the University of Puerto Rico for two years and then started teaching. It was during her second year of teaching that she met Dad. She met him at a U.S.O. dance at Camp Buchanan. Dad's first impression of Mom was that she was shy but she loved to dance. Dad made her laugh and he loved to take her to the movies. She thought he was so handsome in his uniform. After meeting Mom, his heart seemed to be mended.

The moment that Dad announced he was leaving back to the states, she knew she might never see him again, so this convinced her that they needed to get married. So on August 14, 1943, Mom and Dad became husband and wife.

My parents had six children from 1944 through 1956 – three boys and three girls. Mom's job was huge for her, but she always seemed to know how to handle the difficult problems that seemed to always be around the corner. We loved her so much as we grew up and left the nest but we also loved to come home to her. Mom's love was especially seen through the round-the-clock care of her special needs son Harry Leroy.

Another talent that she used for the benefit of the community was her ability to teach English to Hispanic immigrants. When Dad died on February 25, 1989, Mom felt an emptiness, so to fill that emptiness; she found within her a new life of giving to the community. As she grew older, she seemed to blossom into seeing the world as a place to find the good in everything and everyone.

In 1990, she became a member of Fellowship Christian Reformed Church. She loved her church and the community members. She seemed to always want to give back with her talents, be it through her crafts or though her hat shows.

All my siblings and myself, have a very special memory of Mom and we cherish these memories in our hearts. She will be sorely missed but now she is at peace – no more pain, no more worries and she is now singing the praises of the Lord. Rest in peace, dear Mother.

Marjorie Anne Estevis, Ed.D.

Marjorie Anne, or Anne as she is usually called, was born in the back bedroom of her maternal grandparents' home on a cold day in Gladewater, Texas. She and her mother soon moved to Corpus Christi where Estevis was raised. In 1954 she moved with her family to New Mexico, the land of her maternal ancestors.

In New Mexico, Anne began her career in education. She taught secondary subjects in the public schools of Hagerman and Jémez Valley. She also taught junior high reading at the San Diego Mission School on the Jémez Indian Reservation. It was in the Jémez River Valley that she met Coach Francisco Estevis and all the rest is history – a long, long history.

After returning to Texas in 1974, Anne earned graduate degrees in special education and completed raising her three daughters. She retired from the University of Texas-Pan American in 2002. Since then, she has published two novels, two books of young-adult fiction, a short-fiction collection and a book of memoirs.

Anne, a great-granddaughter of John Denver Boggs, Cowboy Poet of Oklahoma, says she never decided to be a writer – it just happened and was a long process. She adds, "Growing up, my generation did not have TVs or electronic gadgets to compete for our time and attention; therefore, we had more opportunity to read, and, in my opinion, all that reading led me to becoming a writer. Unfortunately, I'm not visited by a muse who whispers in my ear, unless it's Andy Rooney; I do feel an urgency to get ideas memorialized on paper. The poem or story won't leave me in peace until I write it."

Birth of a Writer

They told her, "Hush up! Pipe down!
No one cares what you have to say.
Be quiet, time out; keep your lips buttoned
or you'll be sent away."

So the little girl took pencil and paper
and began screaming to the Universe.

A Writer of Essays

After writing five books of fiction in my cocktail-hour years, I think I need a change of genre. Maybe I should try essays, although I must admit essayists never piqued my passions – well, maybe Thoreau just a bit. Perhaps I can become a new-age Lamb or Bacon. I can't even remember the names of many essayists, and my aging brain remembers the names of only two women who wrote essays: J. C. Oates and V. Woolf. I think they were women. They did write essays, didn't they?

My first snag in becoming an essayist is, I think, to write essays, the writer needs to have at least one area of great interest and expertise from which to draw. My forte is educational psychology and, specifically, problems in the learning process. The drawback is there are probably a limited number of readers who really gives a darn why, after so many years, Johnny still can't read, won't read, and probably never will read. I'm losing interest in that debate myself, and find I'm more concerned in exploring how Johnny (who, because of his reading disability, never got an education or a lucrative job) is going to pay for his hospitalizations, medications, nursing home care, transportation, durable medical equipment, and eventual burial now that he is approaching retirement age. Is he going to be heavily dependent on the generosity of our society for those needs? Does he have the same rights to quality care, services, and equipment that those who can read have? And if Johnny is an illegal immigrant (formerly known as an alien), does he have the right to anything? Those questions are fodder for some good essays, I think; however, I shouldn't write about those topics because they are not in my field of expertise.

Another problem I see regarding my area of knowledge is that it doesn't really lend itself to exciting and heart-lifting themes. Furthermore, my style of writing about disabilities and educational issues is clinical and technical and definitely without color and warmth. It took me a lot of rewriting and hard work to beat that clinical stuff out of my fiction writing; I'm not sure I ever want to return to it.

Some might think that I could easily write essays about marriage, homemaking, and mothering. I don't think I have any great wisdom in those areas. It took me several false starts for the marriage thing. And although I've met with some success in marriage (60-plus years total), it has arrived only after I figured out that it is wiser to ride the waves than to make them.

As far as homemaking proficiencies, I had to develop what few I have as I went along flying by the seat of my pedal pushers, so to speak. As a girl at home, I begged my mother to teach me to sew and especially to cook. She balked, saying that she didn't want me dirtying her kitchen, jamming her sewing machine, or scorching her clothes with an iron. She suggested that if I really wanted to learn domestic skills, I should enroll in homemaking classes at school. My high-school counselor told me that I could change my schedule to take homemaking courses, but I would have to drop orchestra. "When pigs play the violin," I responded. All the rest is history.

As it turned out, I don't like cleaning house, washing and ironing, cooking, or gardening. It's too much hard work, and I've done as little of it as I could possibly do and still look at myself in the side of the toaster every morning. I preferred to work outside the home, sometimes holding down two jobs, and always paying a maid to do the dirty work. (God bless you, Carmela, for giving me the last 39 years of your life. We have grown old together.)

Rearing children should be a piece of pizza for me to write about. However, this activity was not my crowning glory according to my mother. She found lots of faults in my parenting skills, and she readily revealed them to me, sometimes redundantly. Well, I had children in my home for many years; it was 42 years from the day the first one came home from the hospital, until the day the last one moved out! My mother had children in her home for only 20 years. (She was cheated out of years because she gave birth to her three children in a five-year span and then sent the youngest one off to boarding school.) I had my children over a twelve year span and in my home for so many years that my chances of making more mistakes than my mother were increased unfairly. I raised my daughters' pets even longer than 42 years.

The last girl out of the house was supposed to take all the animals, but she sneaked away without them.

In my opinion, I didn't do a terrible job raising my three daughters, and I did keep them out of jail. Well, I almost did. One of the little darlings was arrested and taken to police headquarters for questioning, but the shoebox full of marijuana found under the bed in her college dormitory room wasn't hers. Thank goodness!

Even though I can't write about anything other than educational issues, interesting topics for essay writing are numerous. I thought of these: abortion, global warming, illegal immigration, stem-cell research, and same-sex marriage. I have read about these issues, but my problem in writing about them is I haven't established any concrete opinions. My attitudes and thoughts vacillate depending on what I have read, where I have read it (usually in the *National Enquirer*), and how well I felt that day. My thoughts are incredibly more stable on real earth-shaking concerns such as life after death, UFO's, out-of-body experience, Big Foot, and the dangers of traveling across the Bermuda Triangle.

There are three topics about which I have strong feelings, but I don't think I could use them for essay writing. These are politics, religion, and war. As far as politics, I feel a pinch of disgust because I think the two parties are spending too much of their energy in bickering and back-biting. To me, the retaliation displays and posturing of the Democrats/Republicans (choose one) are appearing nonproductive. As a youngster I wasn't aware of Democrats and Republicans. My parents didn't discuss politics in front of children, and they kept their party affiliations and voting behaviors as secret as their sex life (lives?). It didn't matter to me what party supplied the President of the United States; he was my president and a wonderful man regardless. I grieve the loss of my political innocence. Well, I guess our two-party system is better than a one-party system, and certainly superior to a dictatorship. I just wish those people in Washington would shut up, quit bickering, and get to work!

My attitudes regarding religion are complicated for me to explain; therefore, I would have a difficult time writing an essay about religion. This was another topic that my parents (occasional Methodists) deemed too delicate to talk about with children or to discuss in their presence; therefore, I was left to wander through life creating my own personal dogma. My daughters accuse me, from time to time, of being an atheist, or an agnostic, or a pagan. My God (or gods), how dare they! Don't they realize I am not a godless creature, and I sense an omnipotent and omnipresent spirit in everything, whether organic or inorganic? I feel an awesome and inextricable connection to it all, but I don't know how to explain it.

Alas, religion, as well as sex, must remain absent from my repertory of topic options. As for sex, did you know that humans and bonobos are the only mammals that engage in the sex act for pleasure? I learned that recently by watching the National

Geographic channel; therefore, it's fairly obvious I know little about the topic of sex. And it would surely embarrass my children, grandchildren, and my husband to read anything I could write about the subject of sex. My mother would also be embarrassed if she were alive and could still read. I hope her spirit isn't somehow perusing this over my shoulder. Just the thought of it squelches the writing process. It's bad enough I occasionally hear her voice in my head reminding me of my many peccadilloes, but to have her editing my writing is just too much.

The last passion-evoking essay topics about which I can't write are the Iraq War, the Afghanistan War, the Syrian War, and any current or recent wars I haven't named. I can't write about these wars because I don't understand those any better than I understood the Vietnam War or the police action in Korea. (Remember, the one that we hesitated to call a war?)

My war was World War II. I was a child, but I had no problem understanding that one. There were no doubts as to who our enemies were, what they had done to us, and where we could find them. We also didn't have any problems coming together as a nation to do what we needed to do to successfully terminate that war. I don't have any regrets about how we ended it. Those young bleeding hearts that demonstrate at Los Alamos every year make me angry and sad. During World War II, I don't remember any protest demonstrations, any draft-card or United States-flag burnings. If anyone fled to Canada to dodge the draft, I just don't recall that. It was a different era and a different set of circumstances. It was a time about which I prefer to ruminate rather than write, unless of course I use it as a backdrop for my fiction writing. I've certainly done that before.

Speaking of fiction writing, perhaps that is my bailiwick and my comfort zone. That is more than likely where I need to focus my enthusiasm and my energy. As far as becoming an essayist, I really can't conjure up any appropriate topics for myself. I just don't think I have very much to say about anything. Perhaps someday I'll change my mind. As Vonnegut often said, "And so it goes."

My Desert Places

My consorts are the mountains,
my friends the long and languid days.
With nature I am wandering
among inviting yet untrodden ways.
I own the mountain flowers, each rock,
all clouds, the endless skies.
At night the silent forest calms my sleep
with fragrant lullabies.

What more could I desire
than to hold nature to my breast,
Perceive the beauty of the earth
and with her riches be so blessed?
My answering soul cries out that
I have been alone too many days.
My hermitage is long devoid
of human touch and loving ways.

Each day finds me alone,
content but fully not resigned
That you have deemed my kingdom
too distant for you to find.
Our separation is the fruit
of vicious time and monstrous spaces.
I live with only one desire –
to share with you my desert places.

A Change of Rules

By successfully passing written and performance tests in 1950 in Corpus Christi, Texas, I began legally operating a motorized vehicle on public roadways. (Yes, I was just a little girl, but my daddy knew all the guys at the driver's license office.) Since that time, I have passed two more written tests for the state of Texas and two for the state of New Mexico, owing to the fact that I have moved back and forth at will (and sometimes against my will) between those two states. Passing so many tests, of course, doesn't make me an expert at driving, but it should give me a heads-up on knowing the rules of the road.

Apparently, I've been asleep at the wheel for quite some time now because it seems that a few driving rules have changed without my knowledge. This hypothesis is based on observing that some particular "new-rule" behaviors are being manifested by a good number of young drivers (and older ones). I've noted that these drivers had to have taken the Texas written test since I last took it in 1974. So, that tells me that these young people must be operating vehicles from a new body of knowledge and I am just old and outdated. (Avocado remains my favorite kitchen color, and William Shatner is still young and handsome.)

The most common rule change that I have noticed has to do with right-hand turns. This change is two-fold: turning on a red light and turning at a stop sign. The rule required a full stop before executing the turn when I learned to make a right turn on a red light or at a stop sign. Not anymore! Now you just glance to your left and whip your car around the corner to the right. Some drivers slow down, but others don't; there must be an option clause in this rule.

Have you noticed the bike lanes? Have you seen any bicycles in the bike lanes? I think you would have to have a serious death wish to ride a bicycle in the bike lanes in Edinburg. These lanes are misnamed; they are actually "express turning-to-the-right lanes for motorists such as university students who are running late to their destinations". (Perhaps Kevorkian Lanes is a more appropriate designation.)

When there are no bike lanes for the "mad hatters," they create their own lanes from the shoulders of the road. Just try turning right from the correct lane and you may be wiped out by someone passing around you on the shoulder. There's no need to worry if you make those speedy right turns from the shoulder; the police don't seem to care, unless you hit someone. So just go for it.

One of the most frightening changes for me has to do with maintaining distance between your car and the one in front of you. I learned two rules: the three-second rule and the one that requires one car's length for every 10 miles per hour that your car is traveling. These no longer apply. Any time you leave that much space (or any space at all) between you and the car in front of you, just observe how many cars will cram into it. Be particularly aware of the driver (usually a pretty young woman with a phone in her ear) who puts on her left-turn signal and comes up beside you on your right. That means she is going to speed up and change lanes to get in front of you although no space may exist. She has to do this because she is in the right-turn-only lane and she needs to go straight, and she's probably late for class. This young woman is a creative driver because she can generate a space where none exists. To do this, she will first have to rearrange the molecules of your vehicle and perhaps even yours. Just slow down and let her in because she will keep pushing until she either gets in or performs the molecule trick.

Speaking of pushing in, the newest rule for entering the expressway from the on-ramp is to employ your left-turn signal, don't look back, stomp on the accelerator, and go for it. The on-coming traffic will accommodate you somehow. In addition, the pushy drivers will speed around you on the left, and then cut in front of you to make an exit to the right off the expressway. If you look closely you will see that he (almost always a young male) usually has a phone in his ear. I can't help but wonder if these young drivers think they are going to live forever; perhaps they think death is something that happens only to old people, and they are going to be eternally young. (Oh, the foibles of youth!)

There is a new rule, not a changed one, which I observe quite often. It's the young male motorist who appears to be dancing around on his buttocks in the driver's seat, especially when stopped at a red light. His hands are usually drumming on his steering wheel to the beat of a very loud bass that is painfully vibrating your car and your auditory ossicles. The young man appears to be lip syncing. (He never seems to be talking on a phone; it most likely would interfere with his song and dance performance.) You probably won't hear much music emanating from his vehicle, just the loud booming of that bass. The new rule calls for the young man to roll down his windows while playing the music (I'm cautiously calling it music) as loudly as possible so everyone within 500 feet of him will be entertained.

This is also the same driver that goes by my house almost every night at midnight and rattles my windows and awakens me. (Oh well, I usually need to go relieve my bladder about that time every night anyway.)

There are some fairly new rules addressing how babies and children are to be transported in moving vehicles. I say they are new rules because they have come into existence since I was transporting my young offspring in cars, pickups, and vans. My children rode standing, sitting, jumping, or lying on the seat beside me or just bouncing around loose in the backseat.

I am very supportive of the regulations that require the use of seat restraints and infant/child carriers. Undoubtedly there are some folks (derelict parents) who have changed these rules or just don't apply them to their children. I see their youngsters bouncing around in their vehicles, and it is *déjà vu* of the 1970 Estevis family in New Mexico.

As for children riding in the back end of pickup trucks, I don't see as many here in South Texas as I do in New Mexico. (It's probably a New Mexico thing, with women, children, and dogs in the back end and the men riding in the cab.)

Why am I spending time writing about these rule changes anyway? Well, I'll tell you. It's because I am old, somewhat inflexible, and I enjoy exhibiting tirades. (Fit throwing takes the place of things I can't do any more, such as twirling a baton, standing on my head, and sleeping all night without waking up half a dozen times.) Furthermore, I don't like change because consistency is what helps me predict my environment and keeps me grounded in reality. When I awake in the mornings, I want to assume that the earth is still turning on its axis and that a vehicle still has to come to a complete stop at a stop sign before proceeding. If these assumptions can't be met, I may get panicky, and then my imagination will go on fantastic flights of fancy.

Recently, after being cut off at an expressway exit by a young man with a phone in his ear (and, of course, driving a sporty, red automobile), I told my husband that I wished I could invent a ray gun with which I could zap drivers such as the aforementioned young driver. My invention would render the young man's vehicle permanently undrivable, and he would forever have an unexplained and fervent urge to walk everywhere he had to go.

My husband said I was crazy, but he hadn't heard the best part. I told him I wished before I zapped the young man and his car, that I could immobilize his vehicle, and with a long mechanical arm, extract him from his car, and with another mechanical arm with a boxing glove on the end, give him a few punches. My husband said I was nuts. No, I am not, but I am guilty of road rage. I'm also guilty of political incorrectness, but I call them as I see them. (It's my fertile schema at work.)

Of course, I realize that my observations are based on a minuscule sampling of the population of drivers. But don't forget, if enough observers independently provide similar results under similar circumstances, then we are shedding light on something that could be assumed to have validity. And, by the way, some of my best friends are young people (both genders) with phones in their ears, derelict parents, and pick-up-driving New Mexicans.

New Mexico Night

They came– three large, elliptical lights –
and hovered in a black sky above me.
There were no precursory signs of their coming,
 no auguries, no omens; yet they came.
I heard no sounds above the beating
of my heart and the gasping of my soul.

The blueness of their lights bathed me;
and I, holding my infant tightly to my breast,
stood gazing upward, attempting
to rearrange the order of my universe,
trying to reconstruct
a new rationale for my existence.

Then silently they moved away
toward the higher mountains,
leaving me with feelings
of awe, wonder, confusion,
and the profoundest of all –
irrelevance.

I saw them and Frances B. saw them;
even Norma G., who can't see, saw them.
We were not drunk, we were not liars,
we were not crazy, but we saw them
and we know they came.

They were not swamp gas or
Venus or the Virgin Mary;
they were simply three elliptical lights
floating in a midnight sky.
And they showed me with their coming
 that I was nothing more than a clod of dirt
existing on a November night –
somewhere in a river valley –
in the mountains of the third planet –
 belonging to an insignificant star –
at the edge of the cosmos.

They came many years ago
on a dark New Mexico
night and they left. And I –
a lowly piece of nothing –
shouted to the universe,

"Look at me!
              I am here!
                          I exist!"

The Test

The man parked his car in front of a school and turned off the engine. He picked up a manila envelope that was lying on the seat beside him, but dropped it back down. He didn't need to read it again; he knew what it said— 99.99% chance that he was not the father of the child. This was something he had suspected since the beginning, but she had insisted the child was his. He had suggested paternity testing, but she had refused. Now he had had testing done with a company he found online – without her knowledge, of course. Whether or not the results would be admissible in court was questionable, but he looked forward to taking the boy and the test results to her now. There was no reason to wait.

This could be the last time he would have to pick up the boy at school on Friday afternoons. There would be no more summers with the child, no more trips to Disney World, no week-end excursions, and no Little League baseball games. His life would be his own. And the 10 years of child support? What a windfall that would be if only he could get it back from her. Maybe his lawyer would look into that.

The school bell rang and children began appearing along the sidewalks. The man picked up the manila envelope and laid it on the dashboard as the passenger-side door opened and the boy jumped in.

Smiling, the child quickly showed the man some papers and seemed excited to share his class work.

The boy smiled again and touched the man's hand. "Daddy, can we eat at Planet Pizza?"

The man put his arm around the child's shoulders, and pulling him closer, he kissed him on his forehead. "Sure we can," he answered and then took the manila envelope from the dashboard and tossed it into the back seat. He would deal with that another day.

Ancestry

I am the daughter of the hungry, the poor,
The brave Celts, Gauls, and Brits,
Who came to a glorious new world
In crowded, stinking, wooden ships.

And over this land they spread their words –
The brogue, the lilt, and the twang.
I can hear their pipes, their fifes and drums
And the airs their children sang.

I speak their words, I sing their songs,
I am a partner, user, and incorporator.
And I eat their food, I say their prayers.
I am a collaborator.

I am the child of sons of Oñate
Who sought gold, God, and grace
As ranchers, shepherds, and farmers
Along a river of an enchanted place.

I hear their voices; they speak to me
In andaluz, catalán, and castellano
And they sing their songs and dance for me
El Paso Doble, La Zambra, El Fandango.

I speak their words, I sing their songs.
I am a taker, user, and implementer.
I dance their dances and seek their grace.
I am an assimilator.

I see your frowns, I hear your murmurs.
"Who can this woman be?"
So with timid heart, but honest soul
I confess with true humility.

I am one who speaks your words, and sings your
songs.
I am a thief, consumer, and confiscator.
I feel your grief, I share your joy,
And I am an appropriator.

The Pony's Hoof

For days, Maggie had hesitated beginning the chore of cleaning out the storage house in her backyard. But today she had started early and had pulled out dusty trunks, boxes, and old suitcases. All their contents belonged to her – a motley collection acquired over the past fifty years of marriage and child rearing. Most of the items were worthless and would never be used again, but for some reason, Maggie had trouble discarding things she owned. Now that she was a widow with plans of moving into an assisted-living facility, she had to rid herself of many of her possessions. Unfortunately, she would have room for only the bare necessities.

Picking a spot under the chinaberry tree, Maggie seated herself in a yard chair. She placed a nearby cardboard box between her legs and began ripping away the dried and curling packing tape. Upon opening the box, she carefully took inventory of its contents. There were old kitchen utensils, hot-pot holders, oven mitts with crisscross burn marks, and an object Maggie initially did not recognize. She picked it up and held it out before her. It was a small round thing, brownish in color, and looking much like a dirty wad of resin. From it, a small, purple velvet cushion dangled by one thin thread. A wave of recognition suddenly struck Maggie. She gasped and slumped back into the chair, her eyes gazing at the uncomely object.

"The pony's hoof," she whispered to herself. "Grandma Retta's old pin cushion."

How long had it been since she had last seen this thing? At least 30 years she guessed. She faintly smiled, rose from her chair, and tossed the object into the nearby trash can.

All day, as Maggie sorted, repacked, and discarded her possessions, her thoughts kept returning to her grandmother's pin cushion. Finally, she arose from the yard chair and searched through the trash can until she found the pony's hoof with its dangling little piece of stuffed velvet. Returning to sit in the yard chair, she held the hoof tightly in the palm of one hand, and, with the other, forced the velvet cushion into the indention in the tiny hoof.

There – that's how I remember it, she mused as she thought about the first time she had seen the hoof. It had been during Grandma Retta's final visit with Maggie more than four decades before. Maggie and her husband had just moved into their new house, and her grandmother had come to help make curtains and drapes. Memories of that day raced into Maggie's mind. Retta had been alone sewing draperies all day, and she seemed ready for a bit of conversation when Maggie arrived home from work that evening.

"Maggie, come over here please. I have something I want to show you," the older woman had said. She held the pin cushion out to Maggie who took it with a puzzled look on her face.

"What on earth is this weird thing?" Maggie asked.

"It's a pin cushion my mother made from our little pony's hoof. It was such a sad thing that happened." Retta hesitated and slowly shook her head as she took the pin cushion from Maggie. "Yes, such a sad thing to happen to that poor little dear. I was only five- or six-years old – oh, but I remember it like yesterday."

"What are you talking about?" Maggie kicked off her shoes and stretched out on the sofa in preparation for listening to another of her grandmother's stories.

"It was after we had left Medicine Lodge in 1893 and had moved down across the Oklahoma line into the Cherokee Outlet – such a wild and desolate place back then." Retta closed her eyes and shivered before continuing. "My father had gone earlier and staked a claim. Then he came back to Kansas to fetch Mother and his seven children, packing us into a wagon with all our belongings."

"You mean you rode in a wagon?" Maggie asked.

"You bet I did. My older brothers drove the wagon – we had a team of mules. Some of us rode in our buggy which we also had along, but I walked most of the time."

"Why on earth did you walk?"

49

"Well, we children did a lot of walking, and besides, I liked to look for horny toads."

Maggie sat up and looked sternly at Retta. "Ugh, Grandma! Those are scary little things."

"Well, I liked them. I'd catch one and wind twine around and around its fat little body, and then play with it like it was a ball." Retta chuckled.

"Oh, Grandma! That's awful!" Maggie said. "And did your family sleep in the wagon?"

"Oh, yes – just some of us. The wagon had hoops with a wagon sheet so there was some protection. I don't think it took us too many days to travel to our new property. My father was granted a quarter-section – that's 160 acres, you know."

Maggie really had not known that, but she nodded as if she did.

Retta continued, "Our new place was on the Salt Fork of the Arkansas River near a community called Winchester. Umm . . . I bet it's not there anymore."

"And, so how did you live out there on the plains? In your covered wagon – or what?" Maggie asked.

"We lived out of the wagon until my father got us a half-dugout sod house built, and that took a while because he was gone a lot – horse trading, you know – that's what he was – not a farmer."

Maggie yawned and stretched her arms above her head. "Well, I'd better start supper – it's getting late."

Retta quickly replied, "Oh, no – I haven't even told you about the pony's hoof."

Maggie sat up and took the pony's hoof from Retta's hand. "Well – what about it?"

Retta smiled and settled back in her chair. "Well, we had a sorrel mare that had a foal. He was a beautiful little pony, and we dearly loved him. My mother tied the mare near the house at night; she didn't secure the pony because he wouldn't leave his mother, you see." Retta took a deep breath. "One night the wolves came . . . ." Retta's voice broke off and a faint shudder passed through her body.

"Wolves? Don't you mean coyotes?" A wide-eyed Maggie asked.

"No, ma'am. I mean wolves!" Retta countered. "We had plains wolves back then – big, ugly, mean things." Retta seemed to be a bit out of breath. She put her handkerchief to her mouth and fell silent.

Maggie said nothing, but lay on the sofa thinking of what she had in the refrigerator that she could make quickly for supper. She hated to interrupt her grandmother, but she needed to have their evening meal ready when her husband arrived home. Retta's story was taking too long for Maggie, as they usually did. Now Maggie would not have enough time to prepare what she had planned for supper – fried chicken, mashed potatoes, and gravy. Maybe there was enough bread to make grilled cheese sandwiches, and hopefully she would find a large can of chicken noodle soup in the cupboard. Maggie sat up, smiled at her grandmother, and said, "Well, hurry up and tell me – what happened?"

"Oh, my – it happened one night after we had moved into our house, and my father and brothers were gone trading horses. A terrible racket outside awakened us. A pack of wolves was trying to get our pony, and the mare was throwing a terrible fit, and the pony was screaming." Retta stopped, closed her eyes, and cleared her throat. "The noise was horrible – just horrible. That poor mare couldn't really defend her little one because she was tightly tied."

Maggie reached over and touched her grandmother's arm. This was a story she had never heard before. Over the years Maggie had heard many of Retta's stories of life on the plains, most of them repeated numerous times. "Well, did the wolves get your little horse? Where was your mother? Didn't she do something?"

Retta shook her head. "My mother was afraid to open the door. She was alone with too many babies herself to take care of – and besides – she didn't know how to handle a gun."

Maggie quickly interjected, "Oh, how utterly awful! I don't see how your mother could just do nothing,"

"Well, we kids begged her to do something to save the pony. But she couldn't bring herself to go outside." Retta sighed and continued, "The next morning we found the mess. The pony was gone, but there was one little leg left near the house. My mother cut off the hoof, cleaned it up, and dried it – then made this little pin cushion out of it." Retta hesitated. "I guess she thought it would help console us."

"And the poor mare? Was she hurt?" Maggie asked.

"No, but the mare grieved for a long time. She wasn't much good after that because she was so easily spooked. I don't remember what ever happened to her." Retta stopped talking at this point and allowed a tear to stream down her cheek. She had already wiped other tears away with the hem of her apron.

Now, so many years later, as Maggie sat in the chair under the chinaberry tree, she turned the little hoof over and over in her hands. She thought of the pony and the mare and of the mother who took what was left of the pony and had made the pin cushion that Maggie now held. This object was nothing that would be of use to Maggie and there was no reason for her to keep it. She hesitated a moment. Then fighting back a feeling of sadness that she didn't really understand, she gently placed the pony's hoof on the top of the pile of trash in the can and sat back down in the yard chair.

Maggie's mood was suddenly interrupted by the bustle of a woman and a young child coming across the yard toward her.

"Hey, you two! I'm glad you're here!" Maggie smiled and reached out to her five-year-old great-granddaughter. "Come here. Grandma wants to show you something and tell you a story." Maggie quickly rose from the yard chair and retrieved the pony's hoof from the trash can.

The Fresno Tree Above my Car is Full of Black Birds

Their name is Grackle.
They hoot, whistle, cluck, and cackle,
and they rain down excrement
to the detriment
of my white Lincoln Town Car.

I want to take a shotgun
and blast them – every one –
until those dirty little devils drop
upon the splattered top
of my filthy Lincoln Town Car.

My husband says I may be wrong
to kill those birds so full of song.
I tell him to shut his yap.
Those birds are only full of crap
and I see it on my Town Car.

Then I frown and say to him,
"Please get a saw and trim
the branches off the stupid tree
that houses birds that heckle me
and my poor Lincoln Town Car."

He laughs at me and walks away,
but I'm certain that I heard him say,
"It would be much more prudent
if under the tree you wouldn't
park your old Lincoln Town Car."

Rosalinda Garza

Rosalinda, or Rosie as she is often called, was born in Edinburg, Texas, to a Spanish mother and father and raised on a ranch in the Linn/San Manuel area. Poetry and music have always provided a therapeutic outlet for her feelings.

From her grandmother, Rosie learned the value of education, and although born in a poverty-stricken area, she had the privilege of attending two prestigious universities. She is a registered nurse with a BSN in nursing. Rosie worked most of her nursing career at the Texas Medical Center in Houston. She retired due to a medical disability.

Rosie has been writing poetry since she was seven years old and has an extensive collection. None of her poetry took more than 15 minutes to write. She was published in her high school literary magazine, and her work has appeared in anthologies, as well as newspapers. She does not have her own book of poetry yet, but she currently is working on a book that will feature her poetry through different stages of her life.

When I Became the Medium

I bought my first home in Houston, Texas, when I was 25 years old. It was a fixer-upper and located just a few blocks from the Astrodome in an old Jewish neighborhood. The trees were unlike anything I had ever seen – so tall and majestic. My neighbors were mostly elderly widows. I was the new kid on the block. I had a dog and I would walk him down the street. That was how I came to meet my neighbor who was in her 80s. I will call her Ruth.

Ruth had a little dog, too. He was well behaved, and would follow her around the yard and stay beside her always. She stopped me and asked me questions about my career and how I came to buy a house in a neighborhood where there were mostly elderly people. I told her it was in my price range and close to where I worked—The Texas Medical Center. We would continue our talks each time I would walk my dog. Soon, we became friends and she invited me into her home.

She said that she had moved to Houston when she got married and missed her old town of New Orleans. She was wise and made the best candy I have ever eaten. She used a walker and was going blind and deaf. I would often volunteer to go to the grocery store or pharmacy for her since she was unable to drive. Soon, a beautiful and respectful bond formed between us. She loved talking about her life as a ballerina when she was younger. Family pictures adorned her walls and she had china cabinets filled with Wedgwood. Her furniture was well-kept antiques, and she even had a big box filled with a coin collection that she and her husband had collected over the years. Although she had items that were worth a lot of money, she had to stay within a small budget. She said she would never sell anything because each item had been carefully chosen and bought throughout her lifespan. She cared a lot for her grandchildren and wanted to leave them a legacy.

One day, I told Ruth that she had good taste and I knew the items in her house were very valuable, so I felt uncomfortable sitting on the antique sofas and chairs. She just laughed and proceeded to ask me if I wanted to see her most prized possession. I could not imagine what that would be. Ruth took me to her bedroom and I noticed a chest that looked like a pirate's chest at the foot of her bed. There was a large cast iron lock on it. I guess she noticed that I was looking at it because she said, "That's where I keep my most valuable treasure."

I could not imagine what that could be. Her entire house was filled with treasures. I thought that maybe she had some gold or silver bars in there, but I dared not ask. She seemed to notice my inquisitive gestures because she asked, "Would you like to see what I keep so well protected?"

I answered her with hesitation, for I did not know what it could be, but I was curious. Ruth then got the key for the lock and opened the chest. To my surprise, I noticed rows and rows of letters. Each chronicled by date. I asked her who they were from.

Ruth answered with tearful eyes, "They are letters that my father would write to me when I left home."

She continued to tell me how she hated living in Houston and missed her family and former home, but she was married and had to move here to be with her husband. She told me that these letters made her feel better.

I asked her why she trusted me with her secret.

She looked at me with her beautiful blue eyes and said, "I would like you to read them because I sense you are going through a rough patch in your life." She carefully picked out five letters and handed them to me.

I was a little uncomfortable taking them because I did not want to be responsible for them because they meant so much to her. She did make sure to tell me to be careful with them and not spill any coffee on them. I was a klutz. What can I say? She knew that, but she was determined to share them with me.

I took Ruth's letters to my house and placed them on the night stand by my bed and proceeded doing chores. When I was done, I decided to go to bed. I was having a little trouble going to sleep, so I decided to read those letters. I had just opened the first one and before I knew it, I fell into a deep sleep. When I awoke the next morning, I noticed that all the letters had been opened and were lying on my chest. I also noticed that there were two poems written in my handwriting sitting on my bedside table.

I proceeded to read the poems. They were so good and so filled with good advice. Perplexed by what had happened, I quickly got dressed and went to Ruth's house. I read the poems to her and told her what had happened. She smiled as she cried and reached for my hand. She said that they sounded just like what her father would say and asked me if I believed in channeling. I said nothing like that had ever happened to me before, but I could not claim ownership of such beautiful works of art. We both hugged one another and prayed in gratitude for the poems. I gave her the letters back and told her I was going to type the poems out and make them look nice and wanted to give credit to her father. She said he had been dead for over 50 years and that his name was W. A. Lovett and that she was so happy I was doing what I said I'd do.

It was a hard year for Ruth due to medical bills, etc., so she did not have the money to buy her grandchildren anything for Christmas. Then, she asked me to make the poems small enough to fit in a Christmas card because she wanted to give her grandchildren the poems and advice that came with each one.

I did as she told me and made 50 copies of each poem and she gave them to her grandchildren. I had never seen her as happy as she was when she asked me to write something on each card and placed the two poems in each card. She glowed, and her eyes took on a brighter shade of blue.

I still remember that day and the events that led to it. She was like a grandmother to me and I loved her very much. She was gentle and kind. Little did I know that it would be the last Christmas that I would spend with her. She died in the summer the next year, but her memory lives inside of me.

That is the only time I ever channeled poems. I don't expect anyone to believe me, but Ruth and I know better. I know what kind of poetry I write, and this was not mine. If it was meant to be, I was glad to be the medium her father needed to give her and his great grandchildren a new and most valuable legacy. You can find the two poems in my section of this anthology. They are my most treasured poems.

Who do You Propose to Be?

There are people who won't stand up for justice.
Fear has become their guide.
When corruption abounds and others get hurt,
they just run and hide.

There are people who won't use their voice.
Silence has become their chant.
When the innocent ask for help,
they just say, "I can't."

There are people who won't accept responsibility for
anything.
Blame others is what they do.
When the unthinkable happens and it makes the
news,
they say, "It could have happened to you!"

But . . . there are people who are watching,
waiting to take a stand,
people who have morals,
willing to lend a hand.

There are people who are marching.
It doesn't matter if it's cold.
They adhere to their values
and the morals that they hold!

There are people who hear the cries of others.
Their spirit is told to act.
They volunteer to help the helpless.
They are brave, and that's a fact.

So . . . what kind of person
do you propose to be?
One who just talks the talk?
Or one who fights for liberty?

Leaving my Mold Behind

I am but a mass of flesh and bones,
A model of the human race,
A structure doomed to be imprisoned by its own
boundary.

If I could, I would leave my mold behind.
I would set free the spirit that dwells within me.
I would be free!

I would walk through wet cement without
Leaving a trace. I would compose a symphony
Of crickets,
Rustling leaves,
A violent storm surge.
I would float freely on a cool summer breeze,
Have a cup of tea with nature. I would be
Any strand of life,
But not myself.

I would go out just before dawn and see
The day through – a transparent stranger to
All evil, yet, an illusion of good will and love
To a child.

I would be a silent friend to nature.
I would be a secret echoed utterly among
The vastness of the universe,
Afraid of being heard.

Yes, if I could, I would be walking out of my body.
Leaving behind
At the blink of an eye:

Body . . .

Flesh . . .

Blood . . .

Bones

Aching Soul

A simple ray of sunshine singes a naked eye.
A cherished moment of silence,
Broken by a helpless cry.
A penetrating knock beguiling a sacred door,
A soul that aches to speak,
Silenced, heard of no more.
A clock shadows life's uncertain path,
A heart, that once felt love,
Walks now a lonely path.
A childhood memory inescapably seems to fade.
A house, without foundation,
Crumbles where the bricks were laid.
      Crumbling,
          stumbling,
               tumbling down . . .
Like a warrior, madness takes its toll,
Destroying a once fertile mind,
Leaving mere remnants of
The hungry, defeated, humbled,
Aching soul!

Send the Children to bed With a Kiss

Oh, mothers, so weary, so discouraged,
Worn out with the cares of the day,
You often grow cross and impatient,
Complain of the noise and the play.
For the day brings so many vexations,
So many things going amiss.
But, mothers, whatever may vex you –
Send the children to bed with a kiss!

Dear little feet wander often,
Perhaps, from the pathway of right.
The dear little hands find new mischief
To try you from morning 'til night.
But think of the desolate mothers
Who'd give all the world for your bliss.
And as thanks for your infinite blessings –
Send the children to bed with a kiss!

For some day their noise will not vex you,
The silence will hurt you far more.
You will long for their sweet childish voices,
For a sweet childish knock at the door.
And to press a child's face to your bosom,
You'd give all the world for just this.
For the comfort it will bring you in sorrow –
Send the children to bed with a Kiss!

~~~W. A. Lovett
(channeled through Rosalinda Garza)

I Know Something Good About You

Wouldn't this old world be better
If folks we meet would say,
"I know something good about you,"
And then treat us just that way?

Wouldn't things here be more pleasant
If the good that's in us all
Were the only thing about us,
That folks bothered to recall?

Wouldn't life be lots more happy
If we'd praise the good we see?
For there's such a lots of goodness,
In the worst of you and me!

Wouldn't it be nice to practice
This fine way of thinking, too?
You know something good about me . . .
I know something good about you!

~~~W. A. Lovett
(channeled through Rosalinda Garza)

Suanne Goings

Suanne is an artist and poet. She was born in the small Appalachian town of Portsmouth, Ohio. In 2016 Suanne moved to the Rio Grande Valley from Delaware, Ohio. She lives with her brother and nephews in McAllen.

For fifteen years Suanne worked as a reentry supervisor and volunteered as an artist and writer for the Ohio Department of Corrections in both men's and women's prisons. Suanne's art residencies include Columbus Ohio City Schools, The Columbus Museum of Art and The Wexner Center for the Arts at Ohio State University. Also a muralist, she has facilitated over fourteen community murals in central Ohio and Appalachia. She has received numerous honors for her work in the Columbus, Ohio, area including the Arts Freedom Award, the ArtSafe Hero Award, and the Boys and Girls Club Bridge Builder Award.

Since moving to McAllen, Suanne has participated in the NEA Big Read Themed Art Exhibit with the University of Texas Rio Grande Valley and Edinburgh Arts. She has exhibited at South Texas College in the "100 Women, 100 Words" exhibit honoring South Texas Women who have contributed to the Rio Grande Valley and the Dustin M. Sekula Memorial Library in Edinburg. Suanne has been a member of the Write Stuff writing group since 2017.

On January 31, 2002, Suanne's only child Brandi died tragically in an automobile accident. The ongoing journey to transform her grief brings Suanne to her most important artistic and poetic quest yet. Because of this unimaginable loss, she has been stirred to write and illustrate her process in hope that by sharing her experience, she can at once honor Brandi's memory, continue her healing, and offer others on the same path comfort and support. Several of her poems, included in this anthology, are excerpts from her work in progress The Alchemy of Grief – An Artist's Journey Through the Loss of a Child.

Déjà Vu

she gazes out

past the

abyss

wondering what

she's doing

in this lovely

quiet space

with a man

whose only interest

seems to be

himself

she's been there

before

and

doesn't know

how to

not go there

again

Mother and Child

they look
from the shadows
of the sun filled
day
with little perception
what lies
ahead
behind the future
past
a mother's love
and
a daughter's sense
of knowing

Puzzling Over the Mysteries

They come in any shape and form,
In color and in hue.
Disguised in love, in hate, in song,
In pain, and skies of blue.

In thoughts and childhood memories
We mask them if we can.
And in confusion of this play
Does lie the Master Plan.

A Plan so timed and unrehearsed
It seems to not exist.
And thus we find yet many ways
Of which we can resist.

But in the darkness of that night,
A night so long and cold,
In depths of fear and loneliness
The story does unfold.

And piece by piece it seems to fit,
A puzzle, oh so grand,
A vast and wondrous point of view
One touched by God's own hand.

With sight and hope and love and joy,
Look back with new restore.
Let what we see engage our hearts
And whisper "nevermore."

As traveled Souls, we have come far.
That night has come to day.
The Mystic and the Monk converge
In Light not far away.

Across the Distance

We both look out a window view
Into the rising sun,
And know that in the place we are
Another day's begun.

This horizon knows no distance
Or seasons of the year.
It only knows my love for you
And helps to keep you near.

The freshness of the morning sky
Holds hope for days ahead.
Yet still I search for where you are
Remembering what you said.

"Just look for me inside your heart.
I am residing there.
And as the days unfold for us
You'll feel my loving care."

Even in your tender words
My eyes do fill with tears.
As longing seems to fill my soul
The distance seems like years.

Yet in the midst of all the pain
The love I have for you
Is great enough to hold a wish
That life does spring anew.

$\mathcal{F}$ernando $\mathcal{G}$orena $\mathcal{J}$r.

Fernando Gorena Jr., called Fred, was born when the United States was coming out of the depression and before World War II. According to Fred, it was a particularly spectacular time for him to be born. One of his early memories was of his red tricycle. Visualizing his father's truck, he would supply the sound effects as he rumbled around his backyard on the tricycle.

As time flew by, he grew up welcoming new things such as a better home with modern gadgets and an indoor toilet. He has seen world war and new conveniences like radio and television, air planes and jets, and, nowadays, computers. According to Fred, "It's been a wonderful life, at least in my eyes. I may have stumbled a few times but I always got up and marched on".

Fred earned a Bachelor of Fine Arts degree from Pan American University in 1976. He also attended Pan American College way back in the 50s. And while in the service of his country, he attended Ole Miss and the University of Alaska.

Fred enjoyed his four years in the Air Force. While in the service he was a water plant and sewage plant operator and killed "many an enemy." He was in pest control and killed millions. He saw a lot of the country including Washington D. C., Oklahoma,

Mississippi, and Alaska. He loved the latter so much he would have been willing to spend the rest of his life there.

After his stint in the military, Fred had a number of different jobs and says he was happy "most of the time." He ran a grocery store, sold insurance, became a draftsman, and even sold cartoons to Hustler Magazine.

When people find out Fred was in the Air Force, they always ask, "Do you fly?"

He always replies, "No, but I killed flies."

The Big, Black Marble

I loved my Grandfather Chano, a carpenter. He had a big, white moustache and liked to sit on the porch in the swing chair he had built for himself and family. He whittled wooden chains there from a two by four block of wood. I marveled at his strength as the shavings fell on his lap and floor. I could see a link beginning to form.

I once borrowed his knife and cut myself. I never borrowed it again. I was very young then. While sitting with him, I saw the neighborhood kids playing marbles. It was Teddy, my cousin, who was two years older than I and didn't like to play with me because I wasn't old enough. Carlangas and my cousin Chanito, who were the same age as Teddy, were on their knees enthusiastically arguing whether Chanito had fudged on his shot. We called it "foochis."

Carlangas had a big, shiny, black marble and to hit and move that glass ball you must have needed to "foochis."

I got off the swing and wanted to see what was going on. Carlangas was arguing and jumping up and down. I couldn't see because Chanito was in the way. The black marble was on the edge of the circle they had drawn on the ground.

Carlangas' face was a dark brown. He was very dark and he was turning reddish brown because

Teddy's marble, a green, white, and yellow, was within range and it was Teddy's turn. If Teddy knocked the marble out of the circle it was his. The black marble enticingly gleamed and glittered. Teddy planted his hand slowly and aimed carefully. In a blur it rolled and hit the black marble hard and knocked it out of the circle.

I heard the "clack" of marble hitting marble, and saw the look of dismay in Carlangas' dark face. He grabbed the black marble and swallowed it. He was not going to lose it. However, it was stuck in his throat. It was too big to be swallowed.

I called Grandfather Chano and told him what had happened, and he immediately volunteered to do something.

Teddy shouted, "You dirty Messican! You gonna die! It's my marble and you gonna die! You dirty cheater!" Teddy was angry and seemed to barely breathe himself while Carlangas writhed and twisted, choking on the big black marble.

My grandfather grabbed Carlangas face and made him open his mouth, "Let me see, Carlangas, let me see."

Grandfather put his index finger down Carlangas' throat and got bit, "¡Ay, carajo!" he yelled and forced his finger out of Carlangas' throat. Teeth marks were evident on his sore finger.

Grandfather was concerned. That marble could cause the boy's death if it wasn't out of his throat soon. He feared trying to dislodge it, because of the biting experience he'd just had.

Doña Salomé, a local *curandera* lived nearby. My grandfather told Chanito to go get her quickly. She had a certain amount of fame in the neighborhood, and had a clean and good reputation. We, as children, feared her because she resembled a witch, a wrinkled, bent woman with scraggly grey hair and long dresses that often dragged on the ground. She lacked a few front teeth, too. She often sang and mumbled her words as she stirred a boiling pot of clothes, further suggesting she was casting an evil spell.

It was lucky she and her assistant Benito were on their way to visit a patient. Benito had been a patient of hers once. He had been burned over much of his person, including his face. Doña Salomé cured him. The scars never left him, but he considered himself fortunate to be alive, and was now trying to follow in Doña Salomé's footsteps to become a *curandero*.

They hurriedly ran to see if they could help.

Carlangas was turning a purplish brown, still struggling to breathe, as Doña Salomé arrived and said, "Quickly, Benito, cover his ears hard with your hands. Press hard!"

Benito's scarred hands did as they were told.

"*¡Ay, Dios mío!* Help me God to save this child's life!" she exclaimed. She took a deep breath, grabbed Carlangas' cheeks and put her mouth over his nose and blew as hard as she could. Out popped the big, black marble, rolling on the ground.

Carlangas dropped also, exhausted and panting for every breath.

"*¡Gracias a Dios!*" Doña Salomé pumped her fist and celebrated, and Benito's face beamed a scrambled smile.

Teddy, still angry, leaned down and pocketed the black marble. "That's what you get for being a dirty Messican."

I could see Carlangas was happy to be alive and rid of the black marble that almost cost him his existence.

Once I swallowed a piece of tripe that got stuck in my throat and I coughed and pulled it out with my fingers. While in Alaska, a guy swallowed a not-very-well-cooked rind of bacon. Somebody slapped his back and he was cleared to eat more. Then, lately I was in a Mexican restaurant and a fat man choked on a fajita taco. I remembered what to do, but somebody beat me to him and used the Heimlich maneuver. However, in all my experiences, I never saw anyone save anybody's life the way Doña Salomé saved the life of Carlangas.

Firefish

We got ready to spend Monday night on the beach. The atmosphere was warm in the Rio Grande Valley of Texas that September in 1968. A shower had fallen and freshened the earth a day prior.

I've always been in love with the sea. All of us were very excited. My daughter five-year-old Melissa and son three-year-old Freddy already had their bathing suits on. My wife happily fixed about twenty sandwiches for the four of us. I had a cooler with a big block of ice cooling Cokes, Sprites, fruit juices, and apples, and a tray resting atop the ice where the waxed-paper-wrapped sandwiches were stored.

I ran a convenience store at the time and I trusted my brother-in-law to take care of the place while I was gone. It was nothing difficult for him to take over, and I relished the freedom, because I worked there over twelve hours daily. I enjoyed the place, but to me it was paradise to relax on the beach.

My pick-up truck's tank was filled with gas. I had three plastic gallon jugs of water. Everything was ready. The four of us got in, backed up, and drove off to Padre Island. Freddy put his arm around my shoulder and leaned on me while Melissa cuddled against Elva, her five-months-pregnant mother. There were no arguments. Everybody was unusually happy.

The morning was beautiful, although the brightness made me wear sun glasses.

I admired all the dark green citrus trees that lined Expressway 83, and the many fields of vegetables all in evenly-spaced rows. Shortly after passing San Benito, I turned into highway 100 where it was sparsely populated by homes but densely by mesquite trees and cacti. We were getting close now to what I thought was paradise. The road had a slight downgrade as we finally spotted the Laguna Madre. The horizon was a deep blue green and the aroma of the bay, fresh and inviting. Spanish Dagger plants, cacti leaves topped with purple, prickly pears, and brambles of huisache and mesquite formed the foreground.

We drove through Port Isabel to a concrete bridge that crossed the Laguna Madre to Isla Blanca. A swing bridge allowed boats out to the Gulf of Mexico or into the bay. The tires on my pick-up thudded every time we passed over a section of the concrete crossing. It was a narrow two lane road and about a mile long.

We rode down a paved road and found a doughnut shop. All of us somehow had a hankering for that sweet stuff. We enjoyed the ten or so minute brunch; we then took an inlet lane toward the beach and maneuvered down the shore as far as we could go, away from all humanity. My wife and I were satisfied with our choice and settled in, although I'd heard stories of wild coyotes roaming through Padre

Island and rattle snakes slithering over and around the dunes.

While the kids played in the waves, I stretched a tarpaulin over the pick-up, using long thin ropes to tie it to the front bumper and a pair of eight foot long poles to prop up the other end. I set up my cot, which I'd borrowed from my dad, on a four by eight plywood sheet placed behind the truck bed, and arranged the three plastic jugs of water beside a big pan where we would wash our feet. Then, on the truck bed where my wife and Melissa were to sleep that night, I helped unwrap a cushy foam rubber mattress I'd bought in an army navy store. We got ourselves ready for the night. Elva and I then looked after the kids while they enjoyed themselves.

We lunched on sandwiches, potato salad, and soda pop. Melissa wondered why sandwiches were called "sandwich," since there was no relation to "sand" nor "witch." I told her about the Earl of Sandwich. His name was John Montagu, and a man who loved to play cards. Montagu had asked for two slices of toasted bread with a piece of cold meat inside them so he wouldn't get his cards greasy. He didn't invent the "sandwich," they just named it after him. After I had said that, Freddy dropped his twice bitten sandwich on the sand. There was no rescue for it.

We all enjoyed that Monday afternoon. Elva and I sat on the cot under the shade of our tarpaulin while the kids made a sand castle in its shade with a bit of our help when we wanted to. A sweet, fresh breeze blew in from the sea. There wasn't a cloud in the sky and no human crossed our line of sight. I liked our situation – as if we were the only people on earth. The kids were in harmony with each other. They usually argued everywhere we went. Peace was with us.

The sun took its time moving and finally, as if reluctantly, sank into the west, and an hour later we went to sleep. Freddy slept with me in the cot on the plywood, and Melissa with my wife on the foam mattress on the truck bed.

We were so far out we thought nobody would disturb us, but around midnight a jeep with a loud muffler awakened me. The jeep's noise irritated me. I saw its red tail-lights disappear as it went behind a sand dune.

I looked outside our tent and noticed how bright the night was. I didn't remember if a moon was out there. Being careful not to wake up Freddy, I arose from the cot and stepped outside to see the moon, but there was none. I was shocked. High in the sky a million stars blazed away. I'd never seen a moonless night so bright.

The atmosphere was still and quiet, except for the waves crashing forward and fizzling as they receded. I strolled to where the water barely reached me. No wind blew, but the fresh scent of the sea was strong. No seagulls squealed or flew. A blue-grey aura was so surreal it dominated my senses.

I looked up again and saw the clearest midnight I'd ever seen. The planets, the galaxies, and constellations glittered brilliantly. Lustrous whites, blues, yellows, greens, and reds blinked at me. Stunned and grateful, I thanked God for His gift of my sight and life.

I scanned up and down the shore witnessing the incessant waves so rhythmically rolling, folding, and crashing.

A wave lapped at my feet and ebbed as I sensed movement coming out of the tent. Freddy had awakened and toddled toward me. He rubbed his eyes, stopped, pointed upward. "Stars!," he said loudly. "Stars!"

"Not so loud, Freddy. You'll wake up the girls," I said softly, although I would have preferred they see what I had been seeing, too.

Freddy walked past me into a shallow part where miniature waves rolled just below his knees. "Firefish," he whispered. "Firefish."

"Firefish?" I repeated. I looked down and saw flecks of light shining and disappearing just like fireflies. We had seen "glow worms" two nights before in our backyard. I had captured one that had a luminescent lime-green tail and let Freddy hold it in his hand. This time Freddy saw the fluorescent sparks and equated them with the fireflies. He tried to catch one in his hand, but couldn't. I tried, too, and came up with nothing but water.

Whatever the objects were, they kept lighting up and vanishing. I reached down again and again with the same result. It finally dawned on me when I formed a pool in the palm of my hand and the lights wobbled. They were reflections of the stars, the salty water acted like a mirror. I told Freddy about it, and he said, "Stars in my hand," and tossed them back into the sea.

This made me realize that in this universe we were the only two people who had "captured" stars this night. I laughed at the thought. I picked up Freddy, sat him in the crook of my arm and walked out of the water. His wet feet felt cold against my bare stomach. I could have stayed up a bit longer to view the marvelous night sky, but I was tired and sleepy. I stopped on the way to the truck and we both looked up. "How about that, son? Have you ever seen so many stars?"

"No," he whispered, looking at me seriously, his arm around my neck.

I turned and gazed at the sky and faced north, west, south and east. "Wow," I whispered.

"Wow," he repeated.

I carried him back to our tent and dried his feet and hands and then washed and dried my own. I lay down and Freddy followed beside me. His head soon rested on my shoulder. "Good night, son," I said softly.

"G'night, daddy," he told me.

When I woke up that morning, I felt as if the minutes I had spent on the beach that night had been nothing but a dream. But it wasn't. I never saw "firefish" again, but I won't forget them. Not a bit.

Snake and Beans

The sun broke past the highest peak of the distant range of the Sierra Madre. Miguel and Nacha, an Indian couple, awoke at the same time. They had been neighbors and childhood friends until the local priest married them.

He arose from his blanket and *petate,* his palm plaited mat, and walked to the nearby stream, on bare feet over the stones, and stepped into the water.

"*¡Ay!*" he really screamed. "*¡Está fria el agua!* The water is cold!"

Nacha, who silently followed, laughed and replied, "What did you expect, my dear Miguel? A warm bath?"

"*¡Ay, mujer!* I never expected it to be so cold!" he laughed and splashed his face and body with the clear, clean water. "It feels good!"

His wife did the same, "Yes, it feels good," she shivered and agreed.

They had been part of an American engineering company looking for oil in a desert region of Mexico. The Mexican government, however, made the engineers leave because they wanted to nationalize their natural resources. The *federales* had physically chased them out. The pair had stayed after the engineers had hurriedly abandoned them. The two were helpers: while the strong Miguel did the

95

manual labor, the proficient Nacha did the cleaning, washing, and cooking.

They both liked to be alone and together without anyone telling them what to do. They were free. No one, nothing would bother them.

Miguel put on his poplin shirt and trousers, and his sandals that he valued so much. They fit perfectly on his big feet. "What's for breakfast, *mi querida* Nacha?"

"I've got rocks and clods of hard dirt, do you want them boiled or fried?" she sweetly told her husband.

"But what about the beans and rice . . . and the tortillas?"

"We finished them last night . . . and I told you so."

His stomach growled with hunger. He gathered his sling and machete. Miguel looked, and found good-sized stones for the sling, and dropped them in his bag that hung from his shoulder. He strapped on his sombrero, and he was ready,

"Get a fire going, Nacha; I'll get a rabbit or two. I'm very hungry."

"I'm going to wait until I see if you get something for sure," she replied.

She was confident actually that he would bring something soon. Nacha began to prepare by cutting *nopalitos,* new leaf cactus, searching for things she could add to the rabbit he was sure to get. *Chile del monte,* or *chile piquin,* wild hot peppers were prevalent in the desert. There was enough flour, and lard for tortillas.

Miguel entered a small valley covered with dusty, blue-green orbs of tumbleweed. Incredibly to Miguel's joy, a pair of hare's ears stood out over one conspicuous weed. He carefully reached into his bag and pulled out a good stone for his sling. The rock fit perfectly and Miguel began to slowly whirl his weapon and took a step forward to brace the shot in the right trajectory, but in so doing, stepped on a twig that snapped loudly causing the rabbit to jump up in alarm. The stone missed the hare by a fraction.

The animal ran into a cacti laden *chapparal* or thicket not thirty feet away. Miguel slid out his machete and hurried to the thick, miniature jungle of mesquite and weeds. He found nothing but a hissing and rattling rattlesnake. Without a thought he brought the machete down on the rattler's neck. Quickly, he cut off its head. The snake wriggled its last. "Nacha loves snake steaks for breakfast," he said with a smile.

Miguel noticed a vine with blue-green pods that dangled from a mesquite branch. Curious, he opened a pod and found a row of five beans. They had broken purple stripes and seemed to be edible. He took one, and chewed and ate it. *"Poco veneno no mata.* A little poison won't kill," he muttered. The fresh bean was a bit acid, and Miguel wondered if it would taste better if it were cooked. He gathered about fifteen pods, and put them in his bag along with the stones. He skinned and gutted the snake, and put that in his bag, too.

Nacha had found wild tomatoes, onion bulbs, cilantro, and cactus pears with new cactus leaves and had begun to make flour tortillas when Miguel suddenly appeared faster than she expected. "*Que rápido.*" she laughed. "I didn't expect you for another hour or so, *mi querido* Miguel."

"I was hungry, very hungry. I felt I should hurry up, and here I am." He pulled out the snake and showed her his prize.

"*¡Víbora de cascabel!*" she exclaimed. "But what are those sticking to the sides of it?"

"Beans, *mujer*, have you never seen *frijoles* before?"

"But these are different in color and size,"

Miguel thought a moment and replied, "Well, we ran out of beans, so I thought we'd give these a try. Who knows, we may like them and get some more later, eh?"

Nacha stood up from the stool she sat on, "I had cut up some cactus leaves ready to fry, but I'd like to see if the beans would be any good."

Nacha sliced steaks about an inch thick out of the tubular snake. She was happy, because of the anticipated taste, and because she loved her strong, efficient husband.

"Nacha, I think we should be going back to our house. I guess I miss *mi viejita y mi viejito,* my old lady and my old man."

Nacha put a few steaks in the frying pan and watched them sizzle. "I like it here and I'm happy with you . . . all by ourselves with no one to bother us."

Miguel added another twig to the fire. "I do, too, but we're running out of supplies. I am anxious to spend some of this money the Americans gave us."

She smiled at the thought of how nice the men had been to them, and leaving all the good things Miguel and she surely enjoyed, the pots and pans, the tent canvases, the burro, and cans of food which were eventually consumed. The couple even had cots and tents they didn't like to use. Nacha and Miguel preferred the mats on the ground to sleep on and a small canvas for their roof. They were comfortable.

The meal was ready. The steaks were done and the beans were boiled.

Miguel's mouth watered at the sight of the steaming food. They sat at a table and used knives and forks. "Thank you, God!" he said, and she said, "Amen!"

They each ate three steaks and seven bean pods. Their hunger was sated.

Miguel was not satisfied with the beans. "They were too acid."

She agreed, "Maybe I should have cooked them without the pods. ¿Quién sabe? Maybe if given more time to mature . . . I don't know . . . I see you finished them."

"Well, I was hungry, Nacha." He got up and stretched. "I walked a bit far, and I am tired. I think I will take a short *siesta*. When I wake up, we'll discuss going back home."

Nacha went to the small stream and washed the dishes, and pots and pans, came back and comfortably lay down with Miguel.

"Is that you, Nacha?"

"Who did you expect?" she asked and giggled.

Minutes passed. Miguel's sleepy eyes opened to see six-inch, miniature monks dressed in blue-green robes and cowls much like what priests wore, and thick strings unrolling from the long, thin branch that held up the canvas in the small tent. They looked a bit like the beans he had just eaten. The monks were saying things in Latin, holding crucifixes in their right hands as they came down the heavy threads.

Miguel wanted to move to give them room, but he couldn't. He was paralyzed. As hard as he tried, it was impossible to budge. One of them stood on Miguel's nose; his feet were sharp and he pointed his crucifix between Miguel's eyes and said, "*Il Patri . . . Il Fili . . . Il Espiritu Santi . . .* Amen."

Another monk, in a deep voice, moaned, "*Dominus vobiscum.*"

Miguel felt several monks under his body, under his arms and legs as if tying him with the string. His eyes could see what was happening to Nacha. It was what was happening to him. They were pulling up Nacha now. Heaving, and chanting "Amen," with each exertion. Monster toothed faces grinning. "Amen. . . amen . . . amen."

The realization entered Miguel's mind that he was dying. *Not now!* These words he wanted to scream. *Anything, but not this!* But nothing came out of his mouth. *I don't want to die! Please God!* He thought the beans had poisoned both him and Nacha.

Miguel felt being lifted and a tear trickled down his cheek. *I'll be good! I promise I'll be good! I'll go to church every day.* A thread wrapped around his leg abruptly broke, and then the rest of him fell to the mat. He kicked and nudged Nacha.

"I'm awake . . . Did you want something?" she said.

"Nacha! You're alive? *¡Gracias a Dios!*" Miguel hugged and kissed her. "I had a nightmare and dreamt that you and I were dead. These monks came out of the canvas . . . were tying us up with string, and pulling us up."

"Monks? Priests?" she asked.

"Yes, monks, dressed in blue-green frocks wearing cowls, pointing crucifixes at us and talking like the priest does at mass. Nacha, I was crying because we were both going our separate ways. It made me realize how much I would miss you. Promise me you'll always be with me! Never, never leave me!"

"I can do that, I truly love you. I thank God every day that you are my husband, and my best friend." She kissed him back.

A few days later, themselves all packed, and the burro, too, Miguel and Nacha looked around one last time. Miguel finally spoke, "Good bye, my paradise . . . I had a wonderful time. The first thing I'll do, when we get home, is visit the church."

Nacha adjusted her backpack, "Didn't you have a nightmare about those people?"

"Yes, but it was the snake and beans that caused it," Miguel rationalized with a smile. He vowed never to eat snake and especially those beans again.

Hello!

A cockroach skittered over a polished floor
Headed toward the kitchen sink,
Triggered by a constant need for,
A quick, thirst-quenching drink.
He clambered up a cabinet door in a blink,
Expecting no block nor stink,
But when he reached the sink's brink,
A stain near the drain made him think:
"Oh, woe! I don't know!"
An antennae did show just below.
He did approach,
Expecting another roach.
It was, and he looked at she,
And she looked at he.
She smiled, and he smiled much beguiled.
He asked with nothing amiss and a bit of bliss,
"What's a dirty cockroach like you
doing in a nice, clean place like this?"

The Tree and the Old Couple

I was a year older than my neighbor Enrique Solíz who lived across the street. We liked to climb trees. The mesquite on the corner of his lot towered over his house. I would guess it'd be between forty or fifty feet high. Every day when I went to school and came home, I'd see the gnarly, old tree looking so inviting. I'd also see an old couple holding hands, sitting in white-painted, wooden, lawn chairs in the shade. Even when it was scorching hot, there they'd be holding on to each other.

"*Buenas tardes*, good afternoon," I'd say, and they'd repeat my salutation. I must have been nine years old at the time, but I remember them very well. An ancient, gray-haired man wearing a straw hat, khaki pants, a long sleeve dress shirt, along with his wife, in an old-time dress and shawl, and just as ancient, would smile at me

It was a routine for me to go by the house every afternoon, and greet them, and they'd always be there barring rain, cold, or a very windy day.

My schoolmates called Enrique, *La Coneja,* female rabbit. His two front teeth were very prominent, just like Lucila's, his mother. She was, in my opinion, an attractive woman, very active, very vocal, and just a good person. She worked at the packing shed, either slicing tomatoes or grading citrus fruit.

One day while walking home from school, Enrique joined me for the three-block walk. I told him about the tree on the corner of his yard. He said he'd climbed it plenty of times as long as neither his mother nor his grandparents saw him. They thought it was dangerous.

This day it was particularly windy. The old folks weren't in their lawn chairs, because of the wind. Enrique asked me if I wanted to climb the mesquite.

"*Seguro que sí*. Yes, for sure," I said, dropped the books I had brought from school on the grass, and jumped on one branch while Enrique climbed up the other. I was certain I was going to see the water towers of the next towns.

I felt secure the tree would be strong enough; I weighed about forty-five pounds, but I didn't figure about the wind. It made the branches sway from one side to the other. The movement excited me, and scared me from going too much higher. I'd scaled thirty something feet. I could see far down the street, but that's all. Across a big bunch of branches, I saw Enrique had stopped also. Discretion was the better part of valor for both of us.

"*A la chingada*," I said holding onto the swinging branches. "The wind is too strong."

We both climbed down. "One of these days, we'll climb it to the very top," I vowed.

Enrique smiled, "The only reason I wanted to climb it was because my grandparents weren't watching. I'm afraid this was my only chance to do so."

"I guess, I'll wait until then," I replied and walked past my Uncle Ed's place and then across the street to my house. There were plenty of trees in my yard, but not as tall as the one on Enrique's lot.

The days passed by, and soon, months. Every day that I had to walk by that house, Enrique's grandparents incredibly would always be there holding hands. I had to admire them for it. I imagined that there was nothing wrong with the idea. I was a child, of course, and did not comprehend a few facts of life, love, reason, and other feelings.

I was in the fifth grade when Enrique's older brother José, who had been a high school student in Mexico City, enrolled in the first grade. He walked by us as we waited for the bell to begin classes. He wore a bow tie, a sweater, and shoe taps which clicked as he stepped on the floor tiles. It was very unusual to see a teenager in the first grade. In no time at all, he was transferred to high school as soon as he learned enough of the English language to understand the other courses. I lost track of Enrique and his brother after awhile.

Every day, I'd walk by Enrique's house and say, *"Buenas tardes,"* to the old folks. They always repeated my salutation and still held hands. He, wearing the straw hat, and she, with the shawl draped around her shoulders, would smile.

The lofty mesquite tree bloomed with yellow, bottle-washer shaped blossoms. Soon it would be laden with mesquite pods which I sometimes liked to chew and spit out the seeds. I often times remember the striped fruit's sweet taste, but did not like the after taste.

I was about twelve when one day the old couple wasn't in their usual place. I missed greeting them as was my usual custom. I asked my mother about Lucila's parents, and she told me, the old lady was very sick and not expected to live. I could no longer wish them a good afternoon. Maybe Lucila's father would be there.

The next day, the old lady passed away. I remember walking by their yard and not seeing anybody. I felt sad. No longer would I wish her a good afternoon. My mother told me the old man was not feeling very well. He took his wife's death very hard.

While her body lay at the funeral home, the old man died. He couldn't stand his misery any more. Her burial would be delayed for a double funeral. They would be buried together.

I wasn't allowed to go to the *campo santo,* the cemetery. In my mind I'd see the old couple, holding hands and smiling, and I wondered if they would be allowed to hold hands for the rest of eternity. My mother told me they were buried in separate coffins.

I knew about death – that it did occur. I'd lost my grandfather, and my sister. My grandfather was bitten by an arsenic poisoned rat. His hand became infected, and in his late seventies, he couldn't recover. My sister was four when she contracted a fever and died. I was told she was in a hospital. I didn't find out until a few years later.

My grandmother told me that a star came and took my grandfather away. In my mind, it happened. I was six then.

My family liked Lucila. She had always been a good neighbor and she evidently loved her parents very much. I knew Lucila's mother had died of a diseased heart, at least, that's what I was told, but why did the old man die? He seemed in reasonable health.

My mother said he'd died of a broken heart. I had no idea what a heart looked like except for those valentines on February 14th cards. The shattered, jagged, red pieces were all scattered in the old man's chest.

As time went on, I understood about broken hearts, and other facts of life. The years rolled by, I aged, and took a different route to another school then.

I still remember the huge mesquite tree that I never satisfactorily climbed, and the loving, old folks that sat beneath its towering and beautiful shade.

*J*ohn *C*laiborne *I*sbell, Ph.D.

John, like a good many of us, descends from many people, and began life joining his seven brothers and sisters in keeping his wonderful mother occupied. There was never a dull moment. As he grew, he acquired increasingly larger pairs of socks. He saw the world and did a thing or two.

Late in 2011 – which by the way is about the time he met his wife – John began writing a poem a day, a practice he has largely maintained since then. He's published poems in the UK and the United States, but no books of poems as yet, though he remains ever hopeful and has several available for the big day. In a previous life, he published books concerning the Romantic Movement in Europe (which is a passion of his), and some of which are still available.

A visitor to the Valley since 1968, he moved to Edinburg, Texas, with his wife and his son Aibek in 2015, to be near his beloved aunt Frances, a woman of many hats – former Air Force major, Weslaco librarian, and Hidalgo County historian – and also in order to teach languages at University of Texas-Rio Grande Valley. His irrepressible wife Margarita, who like John teaches languages at UTRGV, hears each poem he writes, and invariably tells him it is fantastic. Besides his wonderful students, two things John loves about the Valley are the skies and the birds, which never cease to amaze him. He still has his fair share of socks, including the colorful ones his son gave him just this evening for his birthday, though you will sometimes find him barefoot.

Rio Grande Valley

High-tail it south past Corpus and the King
Ranch to the Rio Grande Valley, as
if Mexico were your goal. And then stop
at the thin string of border towns that stretch
upriver from the Gulf. That's where I'll be.
La Feria, Los Fresnos, San Benito –
some names recall the Spanish land grants, while
along the river, other names retrace
the railway – Edcouch, Elsa, Weslaco.
The rails are here still, and the dusty towns
with their low skylines, and the flocks of birds
that wheel and turn above them. In October,
it's over 90. Palms sway in the clear
blue sky on their long stems. This is the Valley,
where language yields to language. Everyone
drives pickups. Stray dogs chase the trucks, in the
hot mornings, the hot afternoons. The thin
and lazy river marks the border, that
some people cross, and some do not. Beside
a *taqueria*, Burger King. And out-
side town, hot fields of produce. Scrub. The highway.

Privy

The house across the street is almost finished.
This week they've put the roof on, and the holes
where windows go are filling. The front yard
still has the workers' port-a-potty, and
the wooden frame in the garage is not
concealed by drywall. I've no metaphor
in mind here; this is just a house. Last night,
after the workers left, a car pulled up,
from which emerged a family who toured
the site. I was not privy to their talk:
it was a couple, with their kids. I'd guess
the kids were cautioned, and the couple spoke
of what was real and what ideal. This was
no lengthy visit. As I write, the first
construction vehicle arrives, it's just
a little before 8, the sun has breached
the sky's blue confines. Soon, the men will work
on drywall, on the windows. It's a long
day in the sun, they'll need a port-a-potty.

Some Unknown God

The clouds are salmon-pink, along the pale
blue eastern skyline, where at any moment
the sun's gold disk will surface. Here I sit
at my desk, gazing out the window, past
the building site, the rooftops, to the place
the birds are headed. I'd be unsurprised –
I've said before – to see some unknown god
or goddess step out of the brilliant clouds
into our world. For these are full of *mana*,
and that may be what draws the birds, who all
are headed east at sunrise. A stray dog
agrees that it is morning, but in my
neck of the woods, folks are asleep. There's not
a sound that makes it through the double glazing,
as if the planet were on mute. And now
the clouds are vivid gold. The sun is up.

A Country We Cannot Visit

The light of dawn has touched the clouds that drift
above the Eastern skyline. I am not
concerned with shades of pink or apricot
the eye might see at this hour, or the blue
of early morning, when the air is fresh,
and birds cut through it on their journeys. Nor
will I dwell on the building site that sits
just under these clouds, where I look, with its
For Sale signs and its port-a-potty. What
concerns me is the passing clouds that shift
their volume through the heavens. What we build
on Earth is so substantial! That is not
the case in the blue skies, where the tremendous
bright lands and archipelagoes of cloud
we contemplate are liquid and diffuse –
not built to last, but fleeting. They are free
as some great ship unanchored, and that freedom
speaks to my anchored heart. Across the sky's
wide fields, the passing clouds map out a land
we cannot visit, where the buildings lift
their towers and their airy battlements
into blue air. The birds have been there, and
when they descend to Earth, the wings they fold
are cloudy and irresolute, as if
the Earth were not their country. It is dawn
in Texas, where the river meets the Gulf,
and the birds fly, and clouds conduct their business.

Daisy

This morning, Daisy brought a toy and left
it on our front lawn, then high-stepped away
into the neighborhood. I am not sure

what thinking is at work, but Daisy finds
herself on our lawn often. Out of all
our stray dogs, we know her the best. The day

that Animal Protection came to see
if we had a snake in our yard, she vanished,
and reappeared after they left. Our first

day here, she was in the back yard, and felt
the need to bark at us, which is not something
she's done since. Rita feeds her ham, and odds

and ends that Daisy leaves untouched. The cars
that pass get chased. She'll stand by the garage
as we depart or make it home, but at

the roadside, not the door. I often see
her tussling with her peers. They trot or tumble
through the front yards that line our street. The rest

are nameless to us; Daisy we will greet
with brief instructions or commands that she
will mostly follow. She is not our dog.

What the Sun Sees as it Rises

It's almost sunrise. In the Gulf, which lies
some sixty miles from where I sit, the air
is vibrant and marine. The pelicans,
slow-winged, lift into it. The sort of thing
to catch their eye would not catch mine. Below
their drift, the lazy water. It's the time
light filters in to grey the sky, as if
spilt on a table. And between the Gulf
and Europe, daybreak marches on across
the great whales as they travel, and the wings
of aircraft flying overnight, across
the bows of trawler and of tanker, lost
out on the flat Atlantic. This is what
the sun sees as it rises. It's the time
light almost hits the palm trees and the fields
that quilt the land around McAllen, all
the barber's shops, the *taquerias*, all
the morning traffic. I can see the sky
begin to pale above my neighbor's roof,
a stone's throw from 281. You might
just hear a stray dog in the neighborhood,
or see the grackles, knotting and unknotting
as they head east to where the sun is up.

Spell

The latticed fronds lift in the breeze, and come
to rest a moment – lift again. Above
their reaching fingers – blue sky. I am sitting
beside the pool in Edinburg, a place
where not much clocks the afternoon, unless
it be the sun's slow progress, or the fall
of the two fountains' water, or the faint
noise of construction from the Marriott
along the road a spell. *4 FT*, the sign
announces. This is shallow water, and
its surface ripples like shot silk. My wife
is at her Spanish class, a world where hours
and minutes count, where people speak, where you
won't see the palm trees lift above the fountains
in every breath of air, as if they knew
where pollen is, and danced like bees to show it
to my unfocused eyes, beside the pool.

Palm Tree and Counsel

The palms reflected in the pool
are never still; the slightest touch
of air will set them dancing. Much
we know is false, and as a rule

I keep my counsel, like the Fool
in Shakespeare. Verbs and nouns and such
deceive the eye. Put down that crutch
and walk, I tell the vestibule;

some listen, some do not. I might
use words to trace out my delight
at what I see, but won't expect

my language to describe what's real;
that's not its job. These palms reveal
no meaning that I can detect.

Padre Island

The sand in mid-September is so hot
it burns the feet, on Padre Island, where
we came this Thursday. We changed in the car,
and in our haste, missed the red flag which warned
the surf was dangerous. A heron stood
where the waves reached the strand, and spread his
great wings lazily as we approached, to settle
in the low dunes. Sand pipers raced away
across the shallows. A hot day. We swam
against the current, where the waves broke, in
a losing battle, and returned to shore
breathless and wet and salty. Passers-by
saluted us. We ambled down the beach
in our turn, behind a young couple with
their boogie boards conversing with the wind,
slung from a shoulder. It was worth the drive,
and all the sand we toweled off, to swim
a bit in this warm ocean, and to walk
along this shoreline, past the wading birds.

Brilliant Token

The phone lines here neatly bisect the Moon
as it climbs in the East. It is a flat
and brilliant token. We're sat by the pool
in the late evening, just keeping an eye
on how the world is doing. To our left,
the fountains rise and fall. The world appears
to be progressing smoothly, and our job
is not a taxing one. There's little sound
beyond the palm trees' rustle, and the rush
of water hitting water, and our chat.
The Moon's now cleared the phone lines, on its path
through indigo to black. It does a body
good to be sat beside the pool, as night
comes with its train of constellations, all
fresh as if newly polished, and as far
from us as thought, beyond the phone lines' reach.

Weslaco: Street Festival

Dance of Jalisco, dance of Veracruz;
in Weslaco, a little town about
an hour upriver from the Gulf, you may

observe these dances, born in the warm land
of chilis and cathedrals, where the word
for heart is *corazón*. If what you see

is a white dress, or pink and blue, be sure
it will swirl like a wind-blown leaf, and the
people may clap. The men in their *sombreros*

will twirl, and tap their heels, the way a bird
may do when spring is in the air. It is
quite lovely. All this happens in the street;

Texas is blocked to traffic, and the booths
that line it offer food and art, and even
a book or two. A *mariachi* band

warmed up as we departed – violin,
guitar, and trumpet – and a crescent Moon
observed the town, the river, the whole valley,

this mid-September Thursday, when the air
was hot as a warm bath, and friends said hi
in English or in Spanish, as night fell.

Island Out of Season

The season now has ended. As you drive
to the abandoned island, you will find
trucks selling watermelons at the verge

along the highway. Summer's gone. The flights
that brought vacationers have ferried them
homeward again, to northern airports. On

the main drag, everything's on sale, but sales
of boogie boards and flip flops do not fill
the register, the ledger. And the beach

is empty. The waves lap the shore. Along
the waterline, the wading birds will print
their footsteps in the wet sand; and above

the wading birds, you'll see the gulls; but there
are few cars parked at the beach stations, and
no bathers in the water, on the shore,

or wiping sand from sandy feet. The air
thrills to no shouts of pleasure. What you hear
is wind and water, and the keening gulls.

Hugh Jones

Born at the onset of the Great Depression, Hugh M. Jones, Jr. grew up in poverty, beginning his working life at nine years of age and putting himself through college where he earned a B.S. degree in chemical engineering with a minor in mathematics. While still in high school he performed the laboratory work for Dr. Alfred Nier who used the mass spectrograph at the University of Minnesota to prove that turquoise is of organic origin.

Jones worked a number of years in the chemical industry where he contributed numerous articles to technical journals and developed logic diagrams for early computer programs. Later, as a consultant, he performed successful turnarounds of failing companies and was chairman and/or president of four corporations, both foreign and domestic. One of those corporations designed and built one-of-a-kind computers for the personal aircrafts of the Sultans of Brunei and of Saudi Arabia.

During the late 1960s he was a Dale Carnegie instructor in Michigan and Pennsylvania. Among his students were two WWII German soldiers who so loved their time in the United States as war prisoners that they later applied for citizenship and returned here permanently. Their talks were amazing and memorable.

A Korean War veteran, he later lived and worked for 16 years in Mexico. He presently works with revocable living trusts and in estate planning and has several books in progress.

Small Change

"Dammit, Carl, the sonzabitches stiffed me again"

"Whatzamatter, Sunny?"

"It's those bosses from over at the paper company. They come in here for a late lunch a couple times a week and usually don't leave me a tip."

"Don't tip you?!"

"That's right. This place pays me fifty lousy cents an hour and expects me to pick up the rest in tips – if there are any."

"What's wrong with those guys?"

"I dunno, Carl. I'd rather they drove trucks like you. I think those neckties keep the blood all squeezed up in those big brains, and none drains down to their hearts. I need to find a better job."

The door closed behind a small boy, who slid into the booth nearest the door.

"Hang on." Sunny sighed. "Got a customer."

She dragged herself to the booth. The boy was eight or nine years old at best.

"Whatcha want, kid?"

"How much is a chocolate sundae?" His soft voice betrayed his shyness.

"Fifty cents, kid." Her voice was brusque.

The boy seemed unsure of himself, and perhaps here at least was someone she could control.

127

The boy counted the change clutched in his hand. Not enough for what he wanted.

"How much is just a dish of ice cream?" he asked.

"Thirty-five cents. Ya want it or not?

"I'll have the dish of ice cream," he said, taking one last look at his money.

She brought the dish of ice cream, set it down in front of the boy and practically threw the spoon on the table. It clattered loudly as she turned her back and walked behind the counter to talk with the driver.

"Why ya so tough on the kid? He's okay."

"I know, Carl. I'm just so discouraged. I can't make ends meet workin' here, and I'm worried."

"Drivin' truck's tough, Sunny, but it pays good. There's some wimmen drivers out there now. More every day."

"I can't be away. Still have a daughter in high school, and her dad don't pay jack shit to help out. Maybe someday . . . ."

"Gimme that last piece of pie there, Sunny. That looks pretty good."

"It is. Had a piece myself earlier." She lifted the cover and shoveled the pie onto a plate.

Sunny turned and noticed the youngster standing at the cashier's stand. She collected the thirty-five cents from him, and as the door closed behind the boy, she walked to the empty booth to clean the table.

The driver heard her cry out and jumped from his stool.

"You okay, Sunny?" he asked as he came up beside her.

She was leaning over the booth, both arms straight, hands flat on the table. Her head was lowered, and tears fell from her eyes.

There on the table beside a crumpled napkin were two nickels and five pennies.

The Dance

You were with someone, and I was with no one,
Sitting along the wall.
You looked so great, but I had no date
For the lonely high school ball.

You glanced my way, and the tears nearly came,
I had seen you in so many classes,
But I sat in distress in my hand-me-down dress,
Hiding behind my glasses.

Your date for the night was a beautiful sight,
But it looked like she wanted to stray,
For all her attention and apparent intention,
Was focused a table away.

Before very long came a slow, slow song,
And that other extended his hand.
You looked on in surprise as he claimed his prize,
And off she went with this man.

A smile lit your face as you slipped from your place
Were you actually coming my way?
The feeling was strong; it 'twas planned all along,
And I jumped up to meet you halfway.

You swept me along as we danced every song.
It was you and me and the night.
I was then the most beautiful belle of the ball,
As at last everything was just right.

It was there at the ball that it all began,
A lifetime of smiles and tears,
But without a doubt, the smiles won out.
Has it really been seventy years?

The Duel

The small boy writhed in the electric cart, rolled his head toward the ceiling and wailed in frustration. He gripped the controls with distorted hands, his clear mind hobbled by the spasms in his body.

With one eye on her son, the woman quickly sorted through the clothes on the rack, trying in vain to find the right one for her.

Making it easier for them to forget his plight, people turned aside, looking the other way pretending to not notice that the boy was different. An elderly man watched the boy and his mother for a moment and disappeared into the Saturday afternoon crowd.

Suddenly, the old man, on a matching cart, crashed himself headlong into the front of the child's cart. The boy's head jerked forward, then back in recovery, his twisted fingers frantically gripping the handles. The child saw the look of dare in the old man's eyes and squealed.

Struggling with the controls, the boy moved his cart away and charged toward the old man. On impact, the old one swayed about, seeming to nearly fall from the seat.

A crowd gathered, not quite sure how to take this duel between the spastic child and the infirm old gentleman.

The old fellow circled and struck the child's cart broadside. The child jerked uncontrollably as his

133

mother rushed forward to catch him, but she stopped. The look in his eye told her this was his fight, his show. He righted himself, and the crowd cheered. He whooped and struck the old man's cart broadside.

The elderly man sprawled from his seat, landing face up on the floor, his arms extended in defeat. The child howled in delight and rolled his face toward the ceiling in triumph.

The manager, hearing the noise, had just arrived and rushed forward to the old man.

"Leave me alone, young man. Can't you see what's going on here?"

The old fellow got to his feet smiling and placed his hand on the boy's shoulder. The mother, understanding, said, "Thank you sir. My son will never forget this."

The old man looked at her, his eyes moist with distant memories. "Neither will I, little mother. Neither will I."

How to Undo the Stew

Sue and Drew started a caribou stew by their igloo
and asked a few friends they knew to help, too.

Agnew, a cuckoo guru from Seaview, threw into the
stew (on cue) a TV crew from Malibu.

Lulu LaRue, who grew up in a slew near Yazoo, cried
"Yoo-Hoo!" and, with a coo, threw her new blue tutu
into the stew.

A Yahoo named Andrew had ague, went "Achoo," and
blew flu into the brew.

A Hindu named Sabu from Katmandu and another,
too–Nehru from Xanadu – threw a zebu (with moo)
into the stew.

A Manchu from Fuzhou, who grew bamboo, flew to
Honshu, then to Honolulu, Oahu, to Mountain View,
and on through by choo-choo. He used Kung Fu to
subdue a kangaroo for the brew.

A Zulu from Timbuktu, who knew taboo voodoo,
slipped in the dew with his gnu and the two fell into
the brew.

Wahoo, a Kickapoo from Kalamazoo, threw in a Sioux from Tippecanoe. He landed askew and, with a spew, strew stew halfway to Peru.

"Boo Hoo," sobbed Sue. I previewed the stew which I rue through and through. It's pooh stew."

"True," said Drew. "I'd rather chew glue and it tastes like a zoo.

But it's too late to undo the snafu. I knew it was a boo–boo not to review the Manchu. He brought a kangaroo, and you told him to bring a wallaroo."

Adieu

Hugh

The Encounter

High in the Sangre de Cristo Mountains, up where the pine trees clump together in desperate miniature forests, the wind actually sighs as it passes through the branches. It's a sound of tranquility and peace.

For hours, he had hiked through steep, rocky trails to arrive at a lake near the top of the range. Its surface was placid. Not a ripple moved the waters.

Across the lake the mountain, still covered with snow in May, came down to meet the water, leaving its white reflection for him to marvel at. There, on the other side, a mountain lion bounded through the snow.

Abandoning his good sense, the man walked around the lake in the direction of the lion. He had no gun, no knife, no other weapon to protect him but he had to see this magnificent creature at close range.

As he made his way, the bare rocks in the puddles along the side of the lake gave way to deepening snow, and he lost sight of the animal. Approaching the other side, he felt a presence and turned to see the great cat not thirty feet behind him, blocking his return.

Surprisingly, he felt no fear. He stopped and looked at the beautiful creature. The lioness had stopped, too. Sleek and tawny, she watched him with a curiosity mirroring his own as the lake mirrored the mountain.

He knew he could be dead in less than a minute, but his heartbeat was normal. The lioness, too, was calm. Even her tail betrayed no excitement as they studied one another. After thirty seconds, she turned and walked away with an elegance he had never seen in humans.

As the snow deepened, she paused to look back at him one last time. Then she slowly turned again, sadly it seemed, bounded through the snow and was gone.

Only then did he realize that he had known her long ago and would never see her again.

Nostalgia swept over him, and the wind sighed quietly in the trees.

Twelve

Somewhere around the age of twelve, there comes a
pause in the life of a woman,
    A suspenseful time of sunlight and shadow,
        A wait between two worlds.

Will she mask her tender mouth with red and tease
her hair into a great fibrous balloon
    Straining to catch the stance and sound that will
        Stamp her into the
            Likeness of millions just a little older than she,

Or will she be one of the fortunate few who so loves
life
    That she will savor all that remains of childhood's

        Lingering,

        Golden

        Afternoon?

*J*uan *O*valle

Juan Ovalle, a native Texan, was born in Ralls, raised in Donna, and currently resides in Edinburg and Austin. Ovalle is retired from the University of Texas-Pan American, where at various times he coordinated and supervised the English Tutorial Center, the Reading Center, and the Supplemental Instruction Program throughout the years and was an occasional lecturer in the English department.

Ovalle enjoys drawing and painting, especially scenic landscapes. He also enjoys reading and writing, especially science fiction and mysteries. Some of his short stories have been published in *The Monitor's Festiva Magazine* and in South Texas College's literary journal *Interstice*.

Ovalle is currently writing, editing, and rewriting short stories to be submitted for publication once he feels they are ready.

Watermelon Field: The New Guy

Imagine a field full of watermelons. Imagine the rows are a half mile long, and the field is a mile wide. Come picking time, that's a lot of watermelons to be carted away to storage or to market. Estimate at least 200 trucks full, each bringing in around $9,000 – depending on the market – and that's a lot of money that square half-mile of watermelons brings in. Deduct the cost of planting, fertilizing, watering, and caring for the plants; deduct the cost of labor, and deduct the cost of the rental of the trucks and storage, and in some cases the rental of the acreage, and that still leaves a nice lump of profit for the farmer. And that's only for a field half a mile long by one-mile wide.

Major farms rent acreage all over the state. It's possible a farm can have crews working in local fields and also have other crews working in other parts of the state. In other words, a farm can have thousands of acres of produce locally and also have several million acres of crops spread throughout the state, and each area will most likely have local people working the land.

Farming can indeed be big business, so the farmers, or the farm owners, need to have good reliable people working for them in key positions.

These would be the managers, supervisors, and foremen. And the farmer/owner must have quick, clear communication with them. Key personnel must be able to work independently, but they still have to maintain communication with the owners.

No one is more aware of this than the guy who is out there in charge of running the farm. For him, a cell phone is not only a convenience, but also a necessity.

A call from the owner, the big boss, can come any time. He might have last-minute instructions for the foreman, depending on the weather, the market, or any situation that might arise and affect a farm or crop.

For whatever reason, the big boss might decide to move around some of the key personnel, bringing or sending someone from one part of the state to another. So one day, my friend Javier was surprised when the big boss brought over a new guy from the Permian Basin area (Midland-Odessa) to the farm. He explained to Javier that he wanted the new guy trained to be the foreman in the West Texas area. Javier was to show him what he did and how he did it.

Don, the new guy, told Javier that he had worked on a farm before, so he had some experience, but he was surprised at how small the local farms were compared to the ones in West Texas. He added that he was a quick learner and that he was pretty sure he'd pick up what he needed to learn in no time.

One of the first things Javier did was bring out a map of South Texas, and he marked the areas where they had watermelon fields.

"We have fields from Hebbronville to Hidalgo, from Hargill to Rio Grande City," Javier told Don. "And we will go to each one in the next few days so you can see for yourself what exactly is going on in each area."

In the next few days, Javier took Don to all the fields to check on the crops. Don listened as Javier explained that while most people worked eight-hour days, they – Javier and Don – would most often put in 12-hour days with all their responsibilities. He showed Don what to look for in the dirt, the earth where the plants grew. He showed him how to tell when the earth needed fertilizer, when it needed water, when it needed to recover. He showed Don how watermelons were planted so many inches from each other, and how many plants of seedless watermelon plants were planted before planting the ones of seeds. He taught him to calculate how much water was needed per field, depending on the acreage.

"Above all, you have to listen to the boss," explained Javier as they walked down a row of watermelons. He chose a small one and cut it so they could give it a taste test. "Listen to what he has to say, and if you disagree, you need to explain why. He could be wrong in what he's thinking, so you need to explain why you disagree with his thoughts. That's one reason why you need to always have your phone with you. He might call you anytime for this or that, and if this or that is wrong, you have to make sure he knows. A lot depends on things going right, especially when it comes to getting the crops picked at the right time and getting them to market." He noticed that Don did not carry his cell phone. "Where's your phone?" he asked Don.

"Oh, I always leave it in the pickup," Don answered. "No way am I carrying my phone out in the fields. It'll get dirty, and I might drop it if I'm not careful."

"You need to carry your phone; the boss might call you anytime," Javier emphasized. "He might want you to go check out some fields, or he might want you to take a crew to another part of the Valley. You never know."

"He can always call me back," Don said.

The next day, Javier drove Don to the farm's vehicle pool in the morning. He handed Don the keys to a pickup and told him, "I need to go to Hebbronville today. The boss called me this morning and told me to go check the fields to see when the watermelons will be ready for picking. I'll be gone all morning, so you need to go check the ones in Hargill to see if they've been cut and ready to load. Do you remember how to get there?"

"Yeah, it's just one turn to the north from the main road once you reach that small town," answered Don.

"There's a map in the glove compartment in case you need it, but you should have no problem getting there," said Javier as he got in his pickup. "I'll see you tomorrow. The boss wants me to run some errands

146

for him this afternoon, so I probably won't be around. Just check if the watermelons have been cut, and if everything is ready, send a crew to start loading the trucks."

As Javier drove away, Don got in the other pickup and drove toward Hargill. Once he arrived at the field, he left the pickup by the side of the road and started walking in the field on one of the dirt roads the trucks would use, checking to see if the watermelons were cut and ready to be loaded and hauled away.

Don had walked about ten feet when he heard his cell phone ringing. He turned and calmly walked back toward the pickup, but as he reached for the phone, it quit ringing. He put it back on the seat and started walking down the dirt road again. Don was midway down the road when he heard the phone ringing once again. He hurried back but when he reached the pickup, the phone quit ringing.

Don waited, but the phone did not ring again. After a while he began walking through the field, this time going over the rows to see if all the watermelons in all the rows were ready. After he had inspected several rows, the phone in the pickup rang again.

This time Don hurried back toward the pickup, jumping over several rows of watermelons. But he tripped over one of the watermelons and came down hard. He landed on another one and smashed it, getting the juicy meat all over him and, at the same time, ripping his shirt. Don quickly got up and reached the pickup as the phone quit ringing. Frustrated, he carried the phone with him as he checked the rest of the field.

The next morning, Javier picked up Don at the farm so they could go check on the different crews working throughout the Valley. As they walked by a big truck where one of the crews was loading the watermelons, Javier noticed a phone holder on Don's belt.

"You're using a holder now?" he asked.

"Yeah, I thought over what you said and decided you're right; I should carry it with me all the time we're out there," Don replied.

"Good for you." Javier kept a straight face, but he was remembering Don tripping on the watermelon, ripping his shirt, and getting the sticky watermelon juice all over him as he ran to answer the phone in the pickup. From the distance, he would hang up as soon as he saw Don reach the pickup. Yes, Javier kept a straight face, but inside he was laughing. He did, after all, teach Don to always carry his phone with him while he was on the job.

The New Crayons

Tomás was pretty excited when he woke up in the morning. The day before, when they had gone to the store, his mom had bought him a new box of crayons that had forty-eight different colors! The first thing he did after getting up and getting ready for school was open the box of crayons to admire all the different colors. There were so many different reds and blues and greens! There weren't as many browns or yellow, and only three or four shades of orange, but that was okay; he liked the brighter colors more anyway. He took out his old box of crayons – there were only twelve – but they were broken or little stubs that were getting hard to hold when he colored any of the pictures the teacher gave him.

Tomás carefully put the new box in his book bag. Then he went to have breakfast with his mother. He'd go to the school after breakfast and be there nice and early. Hopefully one of his friends would also arrive early, and they'd play on the swings or seesaw until they had to go in to the class room.

The school wasn't far from his home. His mom walked him down a couple of blocks and across the street and there he was. He looked around at the playground for anyone he could play with, but there was no else there. He said "bye" to his mom and started to walk over to the swings.

As Tomás approached the swings, he noticed someone running from around the school building. It was Eloy, one of his classmates, chasing a little girl from another classroom. Eloy was laughing and yelling, and the little girl looked frightened as he chased her down the playground. Tomás had seen the little girl before. At first he'd thought she was the little sister of Rosa, one of his classmates; then he'd decided that she was just one of her friends. But she looked like such a little girl, almost like a baby. And here she was, running away from the class bully. Tomás wondered how the whole thing had started, but as he watched them, she tripped and fell to the ground. Eloy pounced on her, and he started beating her up as he yelled and screamed and laughed. He sounded like a crazy guy.

Tomás ran to Eloy and yelled at him, "¡*Déjala!* Leave her alone!"

But Eloy ignored him and continued hitting the little girl. Tomás swung his book bag and hit Eloy on the head. Eloy turned toward him, but Tomás once more hit him with the book bag. Then he kept swinging the book bag as he chased Eloy away. Finally Tomás stopped as he saw Eloy run to hide somewhere in the building, and he went back to the little girl.

She stood up, her eyes wide as she looked at him, frightened. Tomás approached her and said, "*Ya se fué.* He's gone. *Eloy pelea con todos. Es mejor que te cuides si lo ves.* Eloy fights with everyone. Better watch out if you see him."

The little girl turned and ran away. He watched her run from the school yard across the street to wherever she had come from

Later in the classroom, when the teacher had given the students some papers for them to color, Tomás proudly opened his book bag to take the new box of crayons out. He reached in and brought out a handful of broken crayons.

Seventh Grade

The first day of seventh grade was a totally new experience for me. I was in a new school in a different part of town. Some of my friends and I would probably have some classes together since we'd go to different classrooms for different subjects. I was excited about being in seventh grade.

I walked into my homeroom and took a seat somewhere in the middle of the first row. Soon the classroom was full of students, my new classmates. I looked around and thought I was in a different world. I recognized one or two classmates, but what surprised me the most was that some of my new classmates were blonde. And some of them had blue eyes. There were several who had dark hair, but many of them were blonde. I had never seen blondes before.

Hearing those students talk was like hearing kids on television. They had their cliques and alluded to stuff I didn't know about. I knew I was in a different world when I saw one of them waving an envelope around to show the others a letter he'd received from *Dear Abby*. I was surprised that he had actually written her for advice and gotten a reply. From the fragments of the conversation I overheard, it was a boy-girl problem, but I never did find out what the advice was.

Seventh grade for me was the year that John F. Kennedy was assassinated, and I remember the principal calling everyone to the courtyard in the middle of the school and sadly telling us about what had happened and then dismissing us the rest of the day. It was the year I found out I could read, write, and speak just as well as the native English speakers, and I never worried about that again. When I was asked at the end of the school year if I would like to skip eighth grade, I didn't hesitate taking the offer. But I'll never forget that on my first day of the seventh grade, someone had written to and gotten a reply from *Dear Abby*.

Santa Fe Birthday Club

On Santa Fe Street, some of the women get together to celebrate on each of their birthdays. It started several years ago; at first, several of the women would meet and go out to dinner for their birthdays. Gradually, they started having small gatherings at their homes. And eventually, since there are only a limited number of women and, hence, a limited number of birthdays in the group, they included close friends and relatives and the occasional male into their numbers. Occasionally, I am one of those males for whom they get together for a birthday celebration.

The celebration is either a party at one of the homes or a dinner at one of the local favorite restaurants. At the insistence of one of the women, there is usually live music, and someone will usually bring a birthday cake.

But the real highlight of the celebration is the gift giving – or the gift receiving if you're the celebrant.

There is only one rule for the gift: it must have cost around $10.00 or less (nobody argues if it costs more, though). But there are a few exceptions:

-It can be something handmade, as in some type of craft or artwork.

-It can be a sort of expensive white elephant, something someone owns but doesn't want but that the recipient might like.

-It can be a real white elephant, something that the giver for some reason truly does not want or wants nothing to do with, and so passes it on to the recipient in the hopes it will bring something good to the person and hopefully at the same time put something to rest for the giver. This gift is usually accompanied by a story.

My wife has gift giving for the women down to a science. She'll buy things at around $10 or less all year round when they are on sale, things that are actually expensive, but because of her patience and strategies, she gets them at the cost that meets the rule. She knows the kinds of soaps they like, the kind of costume jewelry they like, the kinds of knick-knacks, candies, movies and music to get them. She knows which colors they like, which scents they prefer, and what they like to eat. And so do the other women on the block.

Maria, my wife, had a birthday a few weeks ago. Once again, we got together at a neighbor's house for a small party. When we arrived, a couple of women were there, and two more women arrived behind us. Once again we sat at the counter while everyone spoke and caught up with the latest around the neighborhood. We had chips and dips. Our hostess told us about another neighbor, a widower who had been seeing a much younger woman and was crazy in love, according to her. She mentioned another neighbor was out of town for a few weeks, staying with her boyfriend who lived in another state.

"What I want to know is, when will I find mine?" our hostess stated. "After all, we used to hang out at the same places; we used to go to the same restaurants. We go to the same church and know the same people. How come they met someone special and I haven't yet? So tell me, when's it my turn? Just don't bring me another sonovabitch."

We all laughed with her.

Our next door neighbor brought out a chocolate birthday cake, and we all sang "Happy Birthday." She brought out a small glittery box and gave it to Maria Elena, saying, "I hope you like these. I saw them and I instantly thought about you."

Maria Elena opened the box and took out some small colorful earrings. She said, "They're beautiful. Thank you very much. They go perfectly with one of my black blouses."

"I knew you'd like them the moment I saw them in the catalogue. I ordered from my niece, who was selling for that company," the neighbor added.

My wife opened another package.

"Oh, I've heard of this perfume," she said, spraying some on her wrist and sniffing it. "It smells very pretty."

Another package revealed a very pretty scarf. An appointment book/calendar was wrapped in still another colorful package.

It seemed that this time, there was no white elephant or story to go along with it.

Several months later, the women decided to have a little birthday party for me this year. Once again we met at our neighbor's house; there were chips and dips, tea and sodas, fruit, fajitas, rice and beans and, of course, cake.

We were all sitting around the kitchen counter, eating, talking, and listening to country music. Our hostess was on a CW kick and liked to listen to it in the background while we were eating. When everyone finished eating, she brought out a chocolate cake, and they started singing "Happy Birthday."

The women started bringing out their packages and handing them to me. Of course, with this group, you have to open the presents while everyone, or most everyone, is still around to see (or hear, I guess) if there's a good story.

One of them handed me a package and told me, "I hope you like this."

I removed the wrapping paper and opened the box to reveal a beautiful Cross pen. By now, most of the women know that I love pens and have a small collection of favorite writing instruments. I thanked her, and another neighbor handed me a gift bag. I removed the colorful gift wrapping and took out a bottle of cologne.

"That used to be my husband's favorite," said the giver. "He used to like it so much that's all he ever bought. When I saw it at the store, I thought you might like it too."

"Thank you," I said, remembering her husband, who had died the previous year.

Another gave me a package of my favorite flavored coffee. I also received gift certificates to the local Whataburger, where I occasionally get together with one or two men from the neighborhood for coffee.

Finally, the hostess brought out a brightly wrapped box and handed it to me, smiling. She said, "Go ahead and open it; I think you'll be surprised."

Wondering what it could be, I removed the wrapping and revealed a box of cigars, but not just any old box of cigars – it was a box of Cuban cigars.

"I know you don't smoke, but occasionally you might feel like celebrating something, something special or some special occasion, and I understand smoking and chomping on a cigar gives you a good feeling of satisfaction. At least that's what the sonovabitch used to tell me," she said, referring to her former husband.

"But . . . but these are expensive," I told her. "They cost a lot more than you should spend for my birthday. What's this box run? About $300?"

"That's all right," she answered, "I didn't spend a dime on them."

She laughed and continued, "They're my white elephant. I don't smoke, and I don't want them around either. Consider them a gift from my ex and me."

"What's the story?" one of the women asked her.

"Well, right before the sonovabitch left me, he had ordered them through one of his friends who can get them with no trouble. He said he wanted them for special occasions. You know he used to like to sit outside with a good cigar and just smoke away. But I think in the excitement of hooking up with his girlfriend and fooling around, he forgot all about them. Anyway, he and his friend were talking, and he gave him . . . yes, about $300 . . . and asked him to get him some special Cubans.

"Right around that time," continued the hostess, "he had met that young girl he says he fell in love with, but I thought it was just one of those things – you know – a midlife crisis.

"Anyway, his friend came over and dropped off the package one morning, and I was going to surprise him in the evening, but that's the day he told me he wanted a divorce, so I forgot all about giving them to him.

"He got a quickie divorce so he could be with that . . . woman, and he just never remembered about them," the hostess said. She smiled and continued, "The other day I was cleaning up and saw the box. I don't smoke, and I don't want them. They're expensive, so I don't want him to have them either. They're mine since I stayed with them. So since I don't want them, I can give them away."

She looked at me, smiling, and said, "And that's how you ended up with an expensive box of Cuban cigars."

The women laughed at the expensive joke on a husband who had done one of them wrong, and I smiled and thanked her for the box of cigars.

I don't smoke, and I really don't like the smell of cigars. I don't know if I'll ever have an occasion that calls for a good cigar. On the other hand, I never really knew her husband; to me, he was just an acquaintance whom I'd met once when we first moved into the neighborhood. If I ever see him around town or somewhere, like at a restaurant, I probably won't recognize him; so I wouldn't feel guilty smoking one of those Cubans.

I wonder what else she'd like to get rid of.

The Collectors

I'm part of a little known group of people called "The Collectors" in this war zone. Nothing glamorous, it's just that we are assigned graveyard duty. I don't know how I ended up getting this assignment. Maybe I got on someone's bad side. Maybe I irritated the doctor on the base. Or maybe it was just the luck of the draw. For whatever reason, I was placed with a group of guys who have to go collect the bodies that, for some reason, are left behind.

Graveyard duty is nerve-racking. We know before we go out what we are going to pick up. We know what to expect. They've been shot, or stabbed, or blown up.

The worst of it for me is that sometimes it might be someone I had known. Maybe not well, but since we are all here in a war area together, we had felt a sort of kinship.

So when we know we are supposed to go on a collection, we prepare ourselves as best as we can. Personally, I try to find a place in my mind where I can separate the here and now and file it away, a sort of separation of all my feelings so that what I am doing feels unreal. Others find different ways to cope. And maybe that's why I had that odd experience.

The base had received a radio call. One of the squads had been pinned down by sniper fire and several of the men were down. There had been a brief exchange and several men had been hit. By the time we heard of it, the squad was returning, bringing with them those they could. But they could not bring all of them.

So the three of us on graveyard duty knew we would have to go out later. When the time came, I felt all jittery since I had not had time to prepare myself. One of the others noticed and handed me a joint.

"Here, this will help you," he said. "I know I wouldn't be able to function without one of these little helpers."

The other guy had already lit up, so I joined them as we drove out of the base. I now understood why they had always seemed so calm before, but it was a new experience for me. My eyes watered; my lungs burned; my throat felt tight. And I started seeing everything all blurry.

Luckily, the maps were quite detailed, and it made locating the ones left behind easier for us. We went back to the base with several bodies.

When we were checking the logs, matching the names on the list and completing the paperwork, I noticed we had somehow overlooked one name, so there was one soldier out there who had not been collected.

"Roll a pair of dice," said my colleague who had given me the joint, "and the one with the lowest score goes out again. It's only one body, so we don't all need to go."

We rolled the dice, and I got the lowest numbers, so I would go out once again. I was not yet feeling quite normal, but I figured that where I was going, it did not matter if my driving was not up to par. I didn't need a map to get where we had gone before, but I did need the map for the location where the soldier had fallen. I parked the vehicle as close as I could; then I walked over to the location marked on the map.

I looked around and spotted an area that seemed to have been disturbed. After taking out a folding shovel, I started moving the sand around. After the first shovelful, I spotted part of a uniform, so I put the shovel away and used my hands; I figured I wouldn't damage the body any more than it was if I used my hands. I was clearing the sand away when he sat up. I jumped back, surprised.

"Jeez, I thought you were dead," I told him.

"I almost was . . . it was close," he told me, "but I got out of the way of that . . . that hand of doom."

"Well, at least I got to you on time; those injuries . . . ." I told him, looking at various injuries on his body. "You're lucky I came back over here to check. If you're able to move, I'll help you to the van; if you're too hurt, I'll radio for help."

"Just let me rest a while longer, ok?" he said. "I feel like I really came close this time." He sat there, looking at the ground.

"You know, I've never heard anyone put it quite that way . . . *hand of doom.*" I mentioned.

He just sat there a while, then said, "We were patrolling this area, but we encountered some snipers . . . I was the last one in the group, behind the others, and I started hearing the . . . the shots. I looked ahead at the others, and as I spotted them, I thought . . . I thought I saw a . . . hand . . . sort of appear in front of one, behind another or besides another, and every time I noticed the hand, it would touch them and they'd fall, dead, so that's why I called it the hand of doom."

I didn't know what to say; I just sat by him and waited.

He continued, "I thought if I avoided that hand, I'd be safe. I kept watching for that hand to appear. Then I started hearing the sniper fire again and the shots kept getting closer to me. Something hit me, but I kept moving, and suddenly I saw the hand in front of me. I moved away from it, and I kept running until I fell there and put sand all over me so the hand wouldn't find me."

He got a faraway look on his face, as if he was not totally there. Suddenly his eyes widened and he looked frightened. He pointed and turned toward me and said, "Look! Look! Over there!"

I looked toward where he pointed and saw what seemed to be an arm materializing in front of us. But it seemed to be coming out of a light floating in the air. An arm seemed to emerge from the light, and then the rest of the man it was attached to materialized. He stood in front of us.

"There you are; I've been looking for you," the figure said. "You've kept me waiting long enough."

I looked at the figure in surprise. He seemed to be robed, covered from head to foot, with a hood covering the face. The whole outfit was white, but what surprised me was that I felt like I feel when I run into an old friend, sort of glad to see someone I haven't seen in a while.

The figure reached for the injured soldier and touched him gently, and I saw that the body was as I had found him. The body had never sat up, had never spoken to me. I looked up and noticed the figure was in front of me now.

A sudden gust of wind blew the cloth over his face as he said, "How about you? Do you want to go with me now? It'll save you a lot of hardships and pain later on."

I looked at the figure, and I felt such a longing, but I knew what going with him meant. "Is it really my decision?" I asked. "I think I'll just wait until my time."

He seemed to sigh. "Very well. I tried to do a good thing here. Just don't try to avoid me like he did; after all, I need to make my collection, too."

He turned and walked away, and as he walked away from me, he became harder and harder to see. I just sat there for a while, trying to grasp what I had just seen.

Later, I heard someone behind me shout, "There he is!" I turned toward the voice and saw the two others on graveyard duty approaching me.

"What are you guys doing here?" I asked them.

"We were getting worried maybe something had happened," one of them said, "You've been gone a long time. Did you run into a problem?"

"I see you found him," stated the other.

"Yes, he was under some sand," I told them. "I had to dig him out. Thanks for checking on me."

"Well, come on, let's get out of here," he said as they placed the soldier in a body bag. They carried the body to their truck as I sat there thinking.

I finally stood up and walked over and got in the truck I'd driven over. We headed back to the morgue, but I kept thinking of what I'd witnessed.

I don't know how long I have left or what I'll live through, but I know that someday I'll see that man appear in front of me.

Isn't just waiting here in the war zone horror enough?

The Ride

Jose loved riding his motorcycle. It was just too bad that his wife did not feel the same way he did about his bike. And he loved zooming in and out of lanes as he passed the cars that always seemed to move so slowly as he rode his bike on the highway. His wife, however, always objected to his driving the bike.

But he did try to pacify her. At least he had agreed to wear a helmet while riding, especially through traffic – and the suit – of course. She had insisted he had to wear not only the helmet but also the padded suit that was supposed to reduce any injury he might receive if, for some reason, he had an accident.

He had to admit the suit, although sort of clumsy, did keep him warm, especially on those chilly evenings and mornings when it was a little cold. And it did help keep the wind chill out. He remembered how he had loved the wind blowing against his body as he drove down the roads, how great it felt to have the air press against him as he drove at a high speed down the highways.

But his wife had given him an ultimatum: wear the suit, or else give up the bike. Of course, she could make his life unpleasant if he didn't cooperate. He did not want to give up riding his bike, so the suit it had been. At first it had been embarrassing to wear it, but then he decided that he did like keeping the wind chill out, and he did think that maybe it was a good idea to have some padding just in case.

He had enjoyed riding his bike to college when he had attended the local university. He used to laugh at the other bikers wearing helmets and padded outfits. Occasionally he'd wear a helmet, but most of the time he'd wear a leather cap along with a leather vest with his regular clothes. But then he'd gotten older and gotten married, and having kids kind of made one think of taking at least some precautions.

He smiled as he zoomed toward Rio Grande City's city limits, where he could at least speed up on the highway for a while. He loved the feeling of zooming past the cars coming from all the little towns along the way. He passed a cemetery on the right and noticed the bright colors of the flowers and adornments here and there where people had decorated the graves.

As he drove past the cemetery, he remembered one of his wife's arguments about him wearing the padded suit and helmet.

"You never know what's going to happen. You know what happened to Ruthie. The poor girl wasn't wearing a helmet, and her face was shattered when she hit the pavement. Do you want your kids to lose their dad if you hit something and fly off the bike at a high speed? You better wear that helmet!"

He silently sighed. He remembered Ruthie. She had been a fun-loving girl who loved to ride on the back of a speeding motorbike. It didn't matter whose bike it was, as long as she was along for the ride. Once she'd taken a ride with him, and he had liked the way she felt pressing herself against his back as she yelled with joy at the feel of the ride, letting the wind blow through her hair. One day she took a ride with the wrong guy. He lost control of the bike as he sped through traffic, and it had cost them their lives.

Before long Jose would pass other cemeteries, and one was where Ruthie was buried. Once again he gave her a brief thought and a silent sigh, and he sped on. He noticed a huge cross on top of a hill, and he remembered a tale his brother-in-law had told him.

"We were going past the cross in Rio Grande City, and the moon was out. I was on my way to drop my *compadre* off at his house, but as we passed the cross, a cloud covered the moon and it got real dark. And then there was a little light as the cloud passed over us and the moon shone through here and there. But with the light from the dash, we could suddenly see a woman sitting between us. She was real still, real quiet, just looking ahead, and she was sort of transparent. I didn't want to turn and look at her 'cause, let me tell you, I was scared. So I kept looking ahead without turning to look at her, and then when the moon came out completely from behind the clouds, she was gone. I looked at my *compadre* and asked him if he had seen her, and he said, 'Yes, but I didn't want to turn and get a good look at her. I have to admit I think I peed my pants.' And he had looked down at his pants just to check himself."

Jose had told him, "The car has separate seats. How could she sit between you two?"

And the brother-in-law had replied, "The pickup has bench seats. She sat between us in the pickup. What, you don't believe me?"

Jose had doubted it; they had probably been buzzed, but he hadn't wanted to upset his brother-in-law, so he said, "A lot of strange things happen on that road."

He passed the cars, zooming in and out between them when there was enough room for his bike, but at the speed he was traveling all he needed was just a second or two before he moved on to another space between cars. He really loved to ride his bike as fast as he could on the highway; it was just too bad that sometimes the police would crack down on bikers driving over the speed limit.

Another cemetery – he thought of poor Ruthie again, remembering how she had felt leaning against him. Another mental sigh – he remembered her from high school, how she had been into weird stuff. She'd been Goth for a while and had been into the weird religion popular with the drug culture. She had believed that some sort of prayer or ceremony could make a person invisible to the police. She had also believed another ceremony would make them invulnerable. She'd settled down since high school, but she had still liked to have a good time. His wife, on the other hand, seemed dull compared to her, not liking riding the bike, not liking loud music, not liking going out dancing anymore like she used to years ago.

Yes, that was the cemetery where Ruthie had been laid to rest. *Such a loss*, he thought. Once again he thought of her riding behind him, with her arms wrapped around him and her pressing against him and just yelling with excitement at the speed they were traveling. Too bad his wife wasn't at least a little like that.

Yeah, Ruthie, I miss you, girl! You really knew how to have fun! he thought as he zoomed past the cemetery.

Lost in his thoughts, he was suddenly aware of something behind him on the motorcycle seat. Puzzled, he tried to look behind him, glancing at the mirror on the handlebar, but all of sudden he felt arms tighten around him, just as he had remembered Ruthie doing. Then it felt as if someone leaned against him, someone or something that felt cold. He shivered.

"Faster, darling," he heard whispered in his ear. "*Más recio, Joey. ¡Dale más recio!*"

No, he thought. *It can't be.*

He felt the arms tighten; then he felt a cold chill on his neck. He glanced at the mirror and saw a headful of silver hair blowing in the night air. He tried to make out a face, but he couldn't. All he could see was the hair. He noticed some white clothing, but he still could not see a face.

"Joey, Joey, Josesito. You've been thinking of me, haven't you? *Te oí.* I heard you, and I came. We can ride forever," a whisper in his ear. "You know *lo que me gusta*," he heard.

He couldn't slow down; the traffic was going the speed limit, and he knew better than to slow down when all those cars behind him were going so fast. But he had to make sure that he wasn't imaging Ruthie sitting behind him.

"There, Joey. Turn there; you know how I love that road," he heard the whisper. He was approaching Las Chinas Road, just west of La Joya, and he remembered driving his bike as fast as it would go when Ruthie would ride with him. There was hardly any traffic there at night, and the smooth paved road was ideal for speeding.

Traffic barely missed hitting him as he turned north at the light without stopping; it was as if something or someone else had taken control of the bike and he couldn't slow or stop. The bike just kept on going at the speed he'd been travelling. He had seen the stadium and had tried to slow for the red light, but the motorcycle just shot down the road that led out to the country.

He glanced at the mirror and noticed the wind blowing her hair all over. Some of the hair blew forward and seemed to wrap itself around his face. He thought it would cover his eyes completely, but then the air blew it away from his face and he just noticed a figure clinging to his back. But did he want to see the face?

174

He looked ahead and everything was dark, with the bike's headlight barely lighting up the road a little way ahead of him. He kept his eyes on the road, watching out for the curves and the little hilly parts that he knew were up ahead.

"*Más recio*, Joey, go faster," he heard the whisper in his ear. "You know *que me gusta tanto!*"

The motorcycle seemed to go faster, much faster than Joey wanted to go, and he started to panic, remembering his wife telling him that anything could happen on those empty roads and no one would know until it was too late. He remembered her telling him to wear the suit, to wear the helmet, but to above all be careful when he was driving.

"*Mira*, Joey," he heard. "Look!"

He noticed a pair of headlights in the distance, and he was afraid of losing total control of the motorcycle at such a high speed. The lights were still fairly distant, but at the speed he was traveling it wouldn't be too long before he met whatever was coming toward him. He hoped it wasn't a huge truck that seemed to take up the whole road.

"Joey, it won't be long. We can be together riding this road forever, *nomas dale más recio*," he heard whispered in his ear. "*¡Más recio! ¡Más recio!*"

The wind blew her hair all over again, toward the back then toward the front, and long strands seemed to wrap around his face again, covering his eyes. He pulled back and tried to guide the bike to the right lane, but he kept struggling with no control over the motorcycle. He looked ahead and noticed the lights were getting close, and he started to panic more. He shook his body, trying to loosen the grip he felt around him and shake the figure off his back and off the bike, but the figure just clung to him harder and harder.

He couldn't identify the vehicle approaching him; his lights only lit up a little of the road ahead, but he knew that it wouldn't be too long now before he ran head on onto the coming vehicle. He hoped it wasn't a truck, not that meeting a car would be much different at the speed he was going.

As the lights approached him, he felt the arms tighten around him more and more, and as he looked ahead, he closed his eyes and thought of his wife and kids.

He heard the rumbling noise as he drove into the lights with his eyes closed, and as he opened his eyes, he realized that he had driven between two oncoming motorcycles.

"Faster. Go faster," he heard the whispering behind him. "¡Dale gas, Joey! ¡Dale gas!" And he felt the arms tightening more and more. He started shaking again, trying to loosen the arms holding him tight, trying to lose the figure clinging to his back, and he let go of the handlebars. Before he realized it, he was heading straight for the stop sign at the intersection of the road he was on with highway 2221. As he saw the sign directly in front of him, he held up his arms in front of him and tried to jump off the motorcycle. Before he knew it, he'd hit the ground while his motorcycle crashed into the stop sign.

After lying on the ground for a while, he managed to get up and look around. He noticed the stop sign was still up but with a dented pole. His motorcycle was on the other side of the highway with the lights still on, and he felt bruised and battered. He looked around, but there was no sign of Ruthie or whatever had been riding behind him. He glanced up at the sky and noticed the full moon shining.

He looked at the motorcycle and noticed it was still in good condition. No great damage had occurred, but the thought of driving back the way he had come and of passing by those cemeteries again somehow didn't seem so inviting. He took out his cell phone.

Later, his brother-in-law helped him push the motorcycle off the pickup's bed, and he pushed it into the garage, still feeling aches and pains from the various bruises. Walking into the house, he told his wife, "You know, Norma, I'm getting too old for this thing. Why don't you put an ad out to sell it?"

Lost Souls

Am I dreaming? I wonder as I walk around Sixth Street, moving among the people crowding the sidewalks at this hour of the night – party people out for a night of frolic, college students looking for a good time, others just looking for any kind of opportunity. No one is aware of me as I move among them; not one notices me.

But then *they* see me, or maybe *they* sense me, and *they* seem to come out of the shadows and follow me as I wander among the crowds. There are so many, calling me now, asking me to help them. I start to panic, feel sweat dripping from my forehead, and suddenly I see her, rushing toward me.

"Danny! Danny! Help me!"

Snapping awake, I realize it had been a dream, but I suddenly have a bad feeling about it. It had felt too much like one of the flashes I'd had years ago. I concentrate, trying to remember my dream clearly. All I can remember was Mel running and reaching out to me, calling my name, panicked.

Mel. I think she's always in the back of my mind, but I hadn't really thought about her in a few weeks. And it has been even longer since the last time I'd seen her. Hesitantly, I reach for the phone on the nightstand and press the dial option, pressing the number one. The phone automatically dials her number as I hold it to my ear, waiting for her voice. After five rings, her phone goes into voice mail. Not knowing what to say, I press the END option.

Lying back on the bed, I try recalling the dream more clearly. I'm not sure if I saw *them.* I'm not certain of anything else, but I am certain I don't want to see *them.*

Lost Souls, Julie had called them. That part of a person that needs to find or make peace, and once that's accomplished, moves on to whatever destiny awaits. *Julie.* No, I can't go through all that again; I hope I have not been seeing *lost souls.*

I call Mel once more, but as before the call goes into voice mail.

Have I been seeing *lost souls*? I recall the last few nights' dreams. In some, I am in a city, like tonight when I was walking along Sixth Street in Austin. In others, I'm by a highway somewhere out in West or South Texas where I can almost recognize the scenery and the landscape. Or I'm in an old part of some city and eventually head toward the newer sections. I think I've been in Laredo, where Mel is from. Once I was in Falfurrias; then I was in San Antonio; now it's Austin. It's as if I've been drawn to those cities in my dreams, and now it seems like *they're* drawn to me. It's as if *lost souls* have been looking for me or I've been looking for *them,* and we've caught up at last.

The phone interrupts my thoughts, and I realize the phone has been ringing for a few minutes. I reach for it and hear Mel, *"Danny!"*

180

Hearing her voice, I awake once again. I'd fallen asleep thinking about Mel.

It is about time for me to get up anyway, so I head to the kitchen and start the coffee; then I go to the bath room to get ready for the day. When I come out, the coffee is ready. As I pour some into a mug, I think about the dream. Once again I call Mel, but as before, her phone goes to voice mail. I wonder if she has changed her number.

Mel, I hope everything is all right with you, I think, visualizing her face.

Arriving at school early, I grab a Dr. Pepper from the refrigerator in the staff lounge, glad to have avoided Austin's morning traffic. But all of that is in the back of my mind. Once again I call Mel's number, but the call goes to voice mail.

"Danny," Mel looks at me sadly, *"I'm sorry."*

I snap out of whatever state I'd suddenly gone into when I hear some of the other teachers coming into the lounge.

Later, as I am lecturing to the class, the principal's secretary knocks at the classroom door and signals me toward the hall. I step out of the classroom, and she tells me I am needed at the office. She adds that she will stay with the class in the meantime.

In the main office, I notice two men sitting with the principal, Mrs. Garcia. She introduces me, and the two, showing me their badges, introduce themselves as FBI agents Bill Guerra and Del Murphy.

"You called Miss Martínez a couple of times from your home and probably a couple of times from the school today," Agent Guerra tells me, "and we'd like to talk to you about that." He looked at Mrs. Garcia, who nodded and stood up from her chair to leave the office.

I replied, "Yes. There's nothing wrong with calling up an old girlfriend, is there? Is this an official, what do you call it – interrogation?"

"No, no, nothing official. We just have a couple of question as to why you called her," one of them answered.

"In that case, I'd like for Mrs. Garcia to remain – as a sort of witness," I state. I'd experienced similar "talks" with officials before. Agent Guerra frowned briefly then looked at Mrs. Garcia, who'd stopped walking out of the office when I mentioned her name, and nodded toward the chair she'd vacated. She walked back and sat down again.

"Anything else? No? Can we get on with this?" asked Agent Murphy.

"You haven't been out of town during the last week or so?" the other one asked, clearly getting impatient.

"I've been to San Marcos and to Round Rock in the last week," I reply.

"Can anyone verify that?"

"I went with Miss Sloss, a math teacher here," I tell them. "What's this all about? It's not a crime to go out of Austin. And what does this have to do with

Mel? Why is the FBI involved?" I glance at them, and then I realize why they probably were there.

"Wait. She's dead, isn't she?" I ask, standing up. "Is that why I've been having those *flashes* about her?"

One of them looks at some notes briefly, then says, "Huh. According to some records, you were involved with some cases several years ago, helping police with what you call *flashes*. Is that what you're telling us, that you've had some sort of insight about Miss Martínez?"

"I'm not sure. It might just have been a dream, not a *flash*," I reply. "I woke up this morning suddenly dreaming her, so I decided to call her."

"Could you explain what you mean by *flashes*? You didn't mean you saw ghosts, did you?" Murphy asks.

I answer, "What I saw were like traces of a person who had died. But I stopped having those flashes years ago."

"So what were they, these *flashes*?" he asks.

"In the 1960s, a Russian researcher managed to photograph people's auras, and since then, instruments have been developed that can measure and verify their existence. I understand that there are even some people who can see auras. For me, having flashes was similar to this," I explain, wondering if they would believe me.

I continue, "When a person dies, the aura doesn't fade away; some type of energy, some type of spark, remains. It's like an echo or reflection of the person. And I could see these reflections and get information from them. Mostly, I think they were like flashes of intuition. That's how I helped in those cases back then, by getting information from what was left behind."

"So you're saying Miss Martínez is dead?" Guerra asks.

"All I said was that I'd had a vivid dream or a *flash* about her, so I decided to call her. So what's going on? Why are you asking me about her?" I ask.

They stare at me for a few minutes, and then one of them answers, "She has been missing for a few days. We believe she has been abducted. The fact that you don't live in the Valley anymore kept you off our list of suspects, but because you were once involved with her and you've called her several times today, it seemed like something we had to look into. You must know why we have to follow up any little thing."

"You mean because of her father."

"Yes; her family expects some sort of ransom demand and want to get through this as quickly as possible," one of them replies.

I'd forgotten Mrs. Garcia was with us until I heard her tell them, "He hasn't taken time off or been absent in the last few days, so there's no way you should suspect him of anything."

"Thank you, Mrs. Garcia. I'm sure they can verify everything easily," I tell her, and turning toward them ask, "Can't you?"

"Could you explain what happened when you saw her in your dreams? Why you called her?" Murphy asks.

"She was running toward me and calling for help."

"Calling for help?" one of them repeated.

"Yes."

They looked at each other briefly, both frowning.

"Well, thank you for your cooperation," Agent Guerra states, and turning toward Mrs. Garcia, he once again said, "Thank you." They get up from the chairs and leave the office.

Looking at the chairs they had occupied but thinking of Mel, remembering her face, her smile, I could *almost feel her* near me.

My thoughts are interrupted when Mrs. Garcia said, "I don't recall anything in your resume about you working with the police."

After a few seconds, I explain, "When I was in college, some girls went missing in the Valley. Somehow I started seeing them, but it wasn't really them. It was like I saw them in quick flashes of time, glimpsing what had happened and where their bodies could be found. I thought I was going crazy, seeing things. I approached a policeman, and explained what I was seeing. He believed me when I gave him names and details nobody else knew. The police followed up on some details I gave them, and they caught the ones responsible."

I wonder whether Mrs. Garcia believes what I was telling her, but continue with my explanation, "Sometime later, a department contacted me about a missing person, a very young boy, and when I walked along a street he was last seen on, I had a *flash* as to where his body would be found. In both cases, my involvement was kept out of the papers, so except for the police and now the FBI, no one else knows. After a while I didn't have any more flashes."

* * *

I'd generalized to Mrs. Garcia. Before Mel, there had been Julie.

I thought I'd been stood up when she didn't meet me as we had planned. Days later, *she* came to me in my dreams. I fell asleep and dreamed of Julie telling me, *Danny, Danny, I really wanted to see you.* I remember snapping awake when she said, *I died,* wondering why I'd dream of her telling me that.

During the next few days, in the mornings when I was waking up or in the evenings just before I fell asleep, I started seeing her in *flashes*, glimpses of her in little snippets of time. I thought I was imagining things. But no one had seen or heard from her in a few days, and, by then, she had been reported missing – she and one of her friends.

One night I had the dream again. And I wondered if it was true, if she were dead. The following evening I saw her, only there was someone else with her, and I could see them clearly.

This time she told me, *Danny, I wanted to see you so badly I'm drawn to you, so please help me,*

186

help us. We can't be at peace until we're found. Tell them where to find us.

As she spoke, two other girls appeared, so there were four of them, and they kept repeating, *Help us, help us, tell them where to find us.*

Julie added, *We're the lost souls, Danny. Help us. Tell them where to find us.*

She touched my face, and I had a *flash*, an insight of where to find their bodies.

Afterwards, how could I not be a suspect, knowing so many details? Ultimately, I'd had to provide details on a cold case in another part of the Valley, a case that involved a prominent member of a community and his family, before my claims of having *flashes* was believed. The insight provided by my *flash* as I walked a city block revealed a body in a back yard, and although investigators were skeptical at first, when they dug in an area I'd indicated, they found the body of a missing child.

* * *

"I know this isn't any of my business, but is Miss Martínez the reason you moved here? To get away from your involvement with her?" Mrs. Garcia asks.

I look at her concerned face and reply, "To get away from the . . . hurt, I guess. I'd always liked Austin and had wanted to move to this area. Mel and I, we'd been together for some time and we'd made plans to move here, but then something changed. She made other plans; she wanted me to quit teaching and work with her father instead. I didn't want that, so we had a huge disagreement about my choices in life and we broke up. Eventually, I moved here."

In the back of my mind I keep hearing Mel cry out, *Help me*.

"Mrs. G., you understand if I take the rest of the week off? I need to go to her. I think I can find her if I can see things the FBI can't, but I need to be closer to her."

She's silent for a couple of minutes. "Just be very careful. You did say that perhaps you were dreaming and that you don't have those flashes anymore."

While Mrs. Garcia was calling for a substitute teacher, I quickly jotted down some lesson plans for the rest of the week. After I turned them in to the main office, I realized I had no idea where to start. To be near Mel, I had to leave the Austin area. But where would I go? Mel's family lives in Laredo, but Mel lives in Edinburg. So if she was kidnapped, it probably happened in the Edinburg area, I reasoned. I drove to my apartment to pack some clothes for a few days.

I arrive in Edinburg about six hours later and drive through the city, finally parking at the Best Western at the southern side of the city. It is pretty well centralized for my purposes. From there, I can hit any major highway that can take me anywhere in the Valley I might want to get to, and maybe in the morning I'll get some idea of where to go.

I check in, and once in my room, lie on the bed and think about Mel. I remember my last words to her.

Once again we had argued about what she wanted of me, and finally, exasperated, she'd told me that maybe we didn't belong together, and I had told her, "You're right; we don't."

I had left her place, gotten in my car, and driven away. I didn't see or call her again, even a few days later when she called and left a message, wondering what I was up to. Days later, when I wondered if I was doing the right thing, it was too late. She'd started seeing someone else.

I'd thought it was all for the best; we were really very different, and then there was her family – I just felt uncomfortable with them being so wealthy, and with her father's office. And now here I was in the Valley again because of her. What was I supposed to do?

Help me, she'd said.

I wonder what to do and if I can actually help find her. Maybe I'll get a flash, some sort of insight. But it's not something I can control and just call up whenever I want.

* * *

Thirsty so thirsty.

"Mel!" I look around, searching for Mel. But I don't even know where I am. Instead of the room at the Best Western, I see a long road in the middle of nowhere. But why are there birds all around me? I'm in the middle of a field full of birds, and they're all looking at me. A few flap their wings and hop forward.

"Caw!" one of them calls.

A few others let out some more caws as they flap their wings. I move away from them and look up and down the road, and I realize it's a highway; it seems to be the one from Hebbronville to Laredo. What am I doing here? As I move, the birds seem to follow me, cawing more and more, and soon all I hear is their caws. They suddenly go silent, but I hear the *other* voices whispering: *help help help help us please please help us help help please please please help.* The birds start flying around me, cawing, and I don't know what to do; I don't know what they want. And where the birds had been, I see *them. They* surround me, asking me for help, and I don't know what to do. I just need to find Mel!

Danny! Hurry!

* * *

I open my eyes to a bright light, seeing her looking at me. I recognize her smile, remembering it. Her smile turns into a frown. *Hurry.*

"Where are you?" I ask, hoping for another flash

She points north then touches my face. There.

A memory surfaced. *I just love coming here,* she'd said. Then she'd stood up and looked at the pond. *Isn't it beautiful?* she'd asked.

I know the place, her family's property a few miles north of Edinburg. I quickly dress, grab my backpack, and rush out of the room. Passing through the lobby, I quickly grab some water and snacks, put them in the backpack, and go to the car.

I drive down Canton Road, hit the expressway, and drive a few miles north until I recognize a road leading to their property. There is a gate with a digital lock. *Birthday*, I sense, and key in her birthday and drive down the road until I see a small building. Leaving the car behind, I feel her near me. I see her and reach to touch her, to see if she is real, but my hand just goes through air.

I walk around the building but don't see anything. Once again *she* stands in front of me, but she is looking toward a trail. Following the trail, I come to a deer blind, a green thing on stilts as high as the tree tops. Climbing up the ladder and looking down, I see *her* looking up and smiling at me. As I look at her, at the essence of the girl I was searching for, she vanishes. Hurrying into the small cabin on top, I see Mel, the real Mel, lying on the floor, her legs and arms tied.

"Mel! Mel!" I kept calling her, as I lift her face and dab some water on her lips. I wipe her face with a paper towel and dab some more water on her lips. I lower her head to the floor then cut the bindings on her arms and legs, massaging them to get the circulation going. I lift her head once again and pour a small amount of water in her mouth.

"Mel, I'm here. Come on Mel, you know we have a lot of catching up to do. Mel, don't leave me again," I tell her, slowly putting a little more water in her mouth.

She opens her eyes slowly, looking at me and giving me a weak smile. "Danny? It wasn't a dream?"

"No Mel, it wasn't a dream. You really came to me somehow," I tell her.

"I'm not dead? I thought I'd died," she whispered. "All I could think of was how we'd messed up."

"I'm here now," I reply as I give her a little more water. After a while, as she slowly sips some water on her own, I use my cell phone to call 911.

She was put on a glucose IV once the EMR vehicle arrived. At the hospital she was diagnosed with starvation and dehydration and continued on the IV.

Later, the two FBI agents who had seen me in Austin arrived and interviewed her, learning the details leading up to her disappearance. They also talked to me, about how I had located her on her family's land. I explained that I had been there before, and with some of the insight provided by my *flashes*, I'd figured out where she was. Her parents arrived, and after talking with the agents, thanked me for helping the FBI locate Mel.

"I'm glad she has a friend like you," Mel's mother told me. "You figured out where she was when there was no clue to her whereabouts and acted quickly before it was too late for her."

"I had to do what I could to help find her."

A friend like you, she'd said. I wonder if that was all I really am.

When others arrive to see Mel, her parents ask everyone to wait in the visitors lounge or come back later since Mel needs to rest and sleep while her meds take effect. I slip out of the hospital and drive to the hotel.

* * *

Julie. I can't believe she actually went out with me. I'm nervous as we drive up to her place after our first date; I don't know what's expected, what to do.

I see the lights on in her place. She looks at the lights, a frown on her face, and she says, "I'd ask you in, but my roommate's there with her boyfriend, and I think it'll be awkward if you meet them at this time. I think they're fighting or something." She leans toward me and lightly kisses my cheek, saying, "I really enjoyed going out with you. Thank you for a nice evening."

Smiling at me, she opens the car door and gets out. She turns and smiles once again then heads toward her place. I'm just thrilled she kissed me.

I watched her get to the door;

I should have walked her, I think. Then I drive home.

At this point I realize I'm dreaming when I see her turn and smile at me again. Instead of going in, she rushes back to the car and gets in. This time, she reaches for me and kisses me passionately, longingly.

"I belong with you, Danny; don't let me go in there," she says, turning and looking at the place frighteningly. I'm puzzled. I know this is a dream because it didn't happen this way. Why am I reliving that evening this way?

"Danny, hold me; don't let me go in there," she says again as she puts her arms around me.

"Julie, what's happening?" I ask; then I feel her arms tighten around me, squeezing me harder and harder. I pull back from her, trying to catch my breath, and as I manage to pull back, I notice it's not Julie holding me; *it's one of them, but different somehow.*

The girl, for it's not Julie anymore, starts laughing and says, "Why didn't you stay with her a while longer? She really liked you; didn't you like her enough to stay with her? Wouldn't you have liked to stay the night with her? You could have saved Julie if you'd shown just a little more interest; it's your fault she died!" She pulls back, not looking anything at all like Julie anymore, and laughs again, saying, "She would have done anything for you."

"You don't know anything about her," I said, pushing her away. "Why are you doing this?"

"Stay away," she says."Don't get involved!"

* * *

"What?" I say aloud as I snap awake. What happened? I feel goose bumps all over my arms as I slowly recall the dream. Is there some meaning to it? Was it a *flash*?

I wonder how Mel is doing. At the hospital, I notice her family looking concerned and keeping a tight lid on her room. I say goodbye to some of the people I recognize and decide to drive back to Austin after all. I should just stay away from her. Mel and I aren't a couple anymore; we've been apart for a while, and I am not sure how she really feels about me. As she said, we messed up. But can we just patch things up and go back to how things were between us?

Driving out of Edinburg, I can't decide which way to go back to Austin. I don't like driving through all the cities on I35, so that leaves about three different scenic routes I can take. Whichever way I decide to go back, it's still a five to six hour drive back, depending on my speed and the traffic in some areas.

As I approach the checkpoint past Encino, I hear a siren and slow down, letting an ambulance with the lights flashing pass me. I notice it bypassed the Customs and Border Patrol station, going through the highway area closed off to the regular traffic. When I arrive at the traffic lanes at the checkpoint, there are a few cars ahead of me, and before long I am on my way again.

That's when I notice the birds. At first it's a trickle, just a few black birds here and there. Then a few more; then it's a flock flying above me. They land on the highway in front of me and just stay there, blocking the highway. I slow the car and finally stop, not wanting to drive through the flock of birds. I notice the exit to Falfurrias is not blocked, so I take the exit and continue toward the city. The black mass of birds takes off to the sky, and before long, the flock is blocking the frontage road at the intersection. The road to Riviera is closed off by the flock, so the only open road is going west. That's when I remember my dream of the birds.

"Am I supposed to go toward Laredo?" I ask no one in particular.

The birds take to the air as soon as I ask. After this happened, what am I supposed to do but head west?

I hear sirens in the distance as my phone rings, and I wonder who would call me at this time of day. The car speakers relay a voice from my phone,

"This is Agent Guerra of the FBI. We met earlier this week. I am calling to advise you to stay indoors. Or, if you can, come to the office in McAllen. We can send someone for you. You are in danger. I repeat, you are in danger and must take safety precautions."

I interrupt his message and reply, "I'm on the road, in Falfurrias at this time. What happened?"

"You might be out of danger if you're out of the Valley. Miss Martínez was taken out of the hospital in an unauthorized vehicle. We believe she has been abducted again by the same people, and we believe you might be a target since you previously located her."

"Wait, don't hang up yet. Was she abducted in an ambulance?" I ask.

After a few silent seconds, Agent Guerra asked, "Another one of your flashes?"

"I'm not sure," I reply. "Not too long ago an ambulance passed me on my way north, and now I've been getting some sort of signs I should head west toward Laredo."

"What sort of signs?"

"I'm not sure I can explain," I reply. I hear a dial tone as the call is ended, then nothing else as the connection is broken.

Past Hebbronville, the highway is long and lonely. Traffic is scarce. Whatever traffic there is rushes past me, mostly pickups and SUVs going well over 85 mph.

I realize I haven't seen any birds since I left Falfurrias, but suddenly I see a huge black spot ahead. As I speed toward it, the spot is getting larger, and I see more black birds landing all around. Pulling over and stopping the car, I get out and approach the flock.

As I near the birds, I notice they're not all black birds, but many different types. And they're all just sitting there looking at me. I approach them slowly, and a few of the birds jump out of the way, creating a path for me.

"You want me to go that way?" I ask, looking at the path. I notice it growing as more birds jump out of the way, and the path leads to a dirt road that ordinarily would not be noticed. I rush toward the road, but when I look back toward the birds, they're gone.

Did I imagine them? I wonder. But I continue on the dirt road, and just past the brush, I see a cleared area in an open field.

Here, here, tell them tell them here, tell them here, here. I am puzzled at the whispers I hear as I look at the field.

An ambulance is parked by a cabin not too far off. I quickly get into the woody area and make my way toward the cabin.

Loud voices come from the cabin. Two men and a woman are discussing something, but I can't make out what they're saying. I use the zoom lens on my phone's camera to make out details in and around the cabin, but I don't notice anything.

As quietly as possible, I approach the ambulance and peek inside. Mel is tied up again, but she's awake. Her eyes widen when she notices me. I put my finger to lips, and she nods. I carefully peek in through the driver's side, but there is no key, so I go to the rear again. I can't hear the voices from the cabin, so I quickly open the rear door, jump in and untie Mel, and then we rush out and start running toward the woody area. As I run, I take my phone out and dial 911.

"How did you find me?" Mel whispers as we rush to the highway.

"The birds," I start to answer, but I feel something hit my back, and I drop the phone.

"Birds?" she asks, giving me a puzzled look. I try to catch up to her, but I toss her my car key and tell her to run ahead and start the car. She gives me another puzzled look but turns and runs ahead. I suddenly feel too weak and too tired to run, and I stumble.

I see Mel look back at me and then start running toward me. Someone in a uniform rushes to her and holds her back and urges her to a vehicle on the highway, telling her he'll pick me up and take me.

I look up and notice the sky turning dark, and then I see *them* around me. There are so many! I stand up and look at *them* as it starts to rain. Somehow, we're all standing in the empty field I'd noticed earlier. *They* look up at the sky and at the rain falling on what I now see is blood soaked ground. The rain is washing away the blood.

I see the girl or woman, the one who taunted me about Julie in my dream, looking frustrated and crying out in anger at the sky. The woman lets out a frustrated scream and rushes toward the ambulance, followed by the two men who had been with her in the cabin.

The birds flutter to the ground. One of them seems to change shape and takes the form of a man dressed in black. He points toward a bright area that is forming, and the birds start cawing and flying in circles, urging *them, the lost souls,* toward the bright light. I look across the field to see if I can spot Mel, but I do not see her, so I start walking toward the bright light, which is drawing me toward it.

She comes out of the light and stops me, taking my hands and pulling me away from the light.

"*No, Danny, it's not your time yet. Melissa needs you and you need her. You have to stay behind,*" said beautiful Julie, the Julie I remembered from the first time I saw her. She smiled and pecked my cheek, as she had that day long ago, and said,

"*Stay here.*" She turned and started walking back toward the light.

"Julie, I'm sorry," I call to her. She turns and smiles at me.

"*Don't blame yourself; it wasn't your fault,*" she says, and walks into the light,

I suddenly wake up in an ambulance with Mel by my side, calling me, "Danny, Danny, don't leave me! Don't you die on me!"

"Mel," it's hard to speak, "what happened?"

"You're awake!" she exclaims, hugging me and kissing my face. "You got shot; don't go to sleep."

"Ok," I say, and black out again.

Sometime later I wake up on a hospital bed and see Mel on the other hospital bed. She had an IV hooked up to one of her arms.

"Hi, Gorgeous," I say.

She opens her eyes and looks at me, giving me one of her dazzling smiles. I remembered one reason I had fallen in love with her.

"Danny? You feel any pain?" she asks.

"No. What happened?" I ask.

"You don't remember?"

"Not really," I answer, but an image of Julie surfaces in my mind.

"What's the last thing you remember?" she asks.

"The field, men shooting, rain," I answer. Then I remember I had a message for the FBI. "I need to talk to Mr. Guerra about some information I received."

Not long afterwards, I explain to Mr. Guerra that I'd had a *flash* while I walked by the field. I close my eyes and remember hearing the voices coming at me, asking for help. I realize what they were asking for. I don't know how many bodies are buried there, but there were many. I had gotten an impression that they had been killed in a type of ritual, but I didn't know why.

Mr. Guerra was skeptical, but he did say they'd look into it.

"So what happened? How did I get here?" I ask Mel once the FBI had left.

"They started shooting at us, and you were hit, Danny," said Mel, "and you went into shock. You started losing a lot of blood, but by then the FBI was close, along with an ambulance. Luckily someone had already called 911 and given an exact location, or else they might have gotten there too late."

"Do you know who called?" I ask her.

"Some girl named Julie, who just happened to be passing by and heard the shots and saw us running in the woods," says Mel. "Besides that, the FBI and the local police were also looking for us. Being a senator's daughter has its advantages. They sent a helicopter and transported us to a Laredo hospital immediately. My father arranged for us to be in the same room. Now all they wonder is how you figured out where I was, again."

"What about the woman and those men, the ones shooting at us?" I ask her. "They're the ones who kidnapped you, aren't they?"

"Yes. They drowned, Danny," says Mel.

"What? How did that happen?"

"All we know is that an unidentified woman and two men were found in an ambulance that had fallen in the river. Their descriptions matched the kidnappers, and some guns were in the back of the ambulance," Mel answers. "Let's not talk about them, ok?"

* * *

Mel's abduction and re-abduction from the hospital had made the national news. Part of the story was that one of her rescuers had gotten shot and was recovering in the hospital. Another part of the story was a mystery: several bodies were discovered buried in the field where Melissa Martínez, the Senator's daughter, had been held right before her rescue by the FBI.

Mrs. Garcia, my principal, was familiar with the facts reported by the local and national news, so when I called her to tell her I needed more time off, she said she understood and told me to get back when I felt I was fully recovered.

In Laredo, I was housed at one of the Senator's apartments while I recovered. Mel had been puzzled why I didn't want to stay with her family in their home, but I explained that I didn't want to frighten them if I had any *flashes* for some reason. Laredo is an old haunted city, I explained, and I wasn't sure if I no longer *flashed* now that she was out of danger.

202

I could *flash* if I concentrated, though. The *flashes* I'd had revealed that Mel was supposed to be sacrificed, especially because of her father. That's why they had taken her to the cabin.

I was puzzled by the fate of her abductors, however. The apartment was near the area where they had been found, so I walked to the location where the ambulance had gone into the river. As I stood there, the images hit me. The ambulance was chased by the local police and the Border Patrol. The driver somehow lost control and the ambulance had gone over the bank and fallen into the river. The impact had knocked the abductors unconscious and they drowned.

I waited for another *flash*. I'd expected a white light to appear for *them,* the drowned abductors, but instead the shadows all around *them* expanded, looking like arms reaching for them. The shadows enfolded *them*, and *they* started screaming as *they* faded into the shadows.

I smiled and walked away.

* * *

I avoid Mel. I remember our arguments and that she had started seeing someone else. I did not want to go through all of that again. She loves her family and especially her father very much. I know that eventually we'll go back to our old arguments about my choices in life.

"You're an idiot," she says when I explain all of this to her. She's come to the apartment to spend time with me and to start planning our future. She stands up and leaves. The next day, I leave Laredo.

* * *

Once I drive out of the Laredo area, I feel different. I felt free of the flashes that infringed on my consciousness. Maybe something about the south Texas area affects me, so I am especially glad to leave. My one regret is that Mel is no longer in my life again. Different backgrounds, different lifestyles, different points of view – we were just too different. I am happy that Mel is all right in spite of being abducted twice.

In actuality, I have not been gone too long from the school, so I easily get back to my work routine. Mrs. Garcia had not told any of the staff about my involvement with the case of the Senator's daughter, so most people assumed I had been in an accident that kept me bedridden and recovering for a few days. I'd received several get well cards from students and staff while I was out. That brightened my day when I saw them. My life is almost back to normal, but I feel something missing from my life.

Days later, the apartment manager meets me as I walk to my apartment after school and says,

"She's as pretty as that weather girl on TV! She said she wanted to surprise you, so I let her into your place since she didn't have a key. I hope you don't mind."

"Who are you talking about?" I ask.

"Your fiancé! I didn't know you even had a girlfriend!" he replies.

My what? What's he talking about? What weather girl? I wonder as I walked into the apartment. I notice some suitcases by the sofa and Mel rushing toward me, smiling. After kissing me, she says, "Let's get married. Soon."

"Mel, think about what you're doing. Do you really think you'd be happy with me? Would you really want to live here?"

"Like I told you in my dream," she said, "we messed up. When I thought I was going to die, you were all I could think of. If you're happy living and teaching in Austin, I'll be happy here with you." After a few minutes, she adds, "My father told me I should be happy that you do not want to base your life on his career, and that you can be counted on when something needs to be done. Otherwise, why would you look for me on your own and find me when even the FBI had no clue as to where I was? And you did it twice! He admires that about you."

The FBI agents came to see us a few days after Mel moved in with me. There were a few details they had to clear up about the Laredo incident. One of them finally asked me, "So how did you really find her? How did you end up in that field?"

I explain, "She thought she was dying. I kept flashing on that, and that led me to her. At least, that's what I think happened. The second time, I'm not sure exactly what happened, but I was led to that field. I think that some things happen that seem to have no logical explanation. My feeling is . . ."

"Is what?" Mr. Guerra asks after I hesitated stating my thought.

"There's something else going on right below the surface. I mean, something that we can't really see happening. How are sacrificial rituals and shape shifting birds connected?"

"Shape shifting birds?"

"Forget it; it was just a dream I had," I told him. "But I get the feeling that, that there's something we're not seeing."

"Well," he explains after a while, "we caught the people behind her abduction. It involved more than those three who drowned. I don't think you'll have to worry about anyone coming after her, or you, anymore," he said. "Unfortunately, the senator has other enemies out there."

Several weeks later, Mel and I settle into our new house. One morning, as I wake to a bright morning light, I look at Mel and follow her gaze. I focus on the point of light she was looking at. A *young girl was looking at us.* I realize that after her experience, Mel was experiencing the same flashes I glimpse.

"Help me," cries the girl.

Gloria Perez

Gloria Perez is a short story writer with an old soul. She's a walking contradiction, and an artist in her mind. She was born into the life of a nomad, finally settling in Texas with her dogs, Sukkie Monkee and Rosé Day, a rescued Shorkie and Shih Tzu, respectively. She collects stories from her travels, and is inspired by world myths, classic fairy tales, and human superstition. Gloria is working to complete her first short story collection. Find her on Instagram @lethean_tales and Twitter @letheantales.

Rest in Peace, First Love

She was humiliated. Belinda had put her heart out there in a nonchalant text, but now she suspected that she had became just another victim of the dating game. It had been two days without a response.

It was her pride that hurt more than her heart, but the new addition to the clutter of silver hairs on top of her head, reminded her that she needed to stop running and take a chance. It was a lousy start to the game, and she knew that another rejection would put her out of commission. Her heart was weak, and after each rejection she became self-destructive. She wasn't trying hard to get a date, but the few attempts she made had been disappointing. At thirty-one she thought of giving love a second chance, but it was turning out to be unnecessarily hard work.

She had often wondered where the romantic schoolgirl she once was had gone. Belinda had been a girl that read romance novels at every opportunity. Once she had dreamed of finding her Fitzwilliam Darcy, a loyal and thoughtful partner, but, somewhere along the line, she decided to settle for a George Wickham, a handsome opportunist. Years later, a cynical shell of a daydreamer was left behind in silent solitude. She could go days without hearing her own voice. Belinda needed to prove that the girl once existed and ran to her closet to look for her box of high school photos. There she found photos of a younger version of her face smiling with her high school friends, eating sweets she can no longer consume, and embracing her first love. She kept pictures of Koji Takano, her high school sweetheart out of sight but, apparently, she had missed one.

Koji had been Belinda's first love, and maybe only love. She had always admitted to herself that she compared every suitor to Koji, and no one came close to him. Koji was special, and the first boy that made her heart beat wild every time he moved near her. He was intelligent and considerate. He always put her happiness before his. Koji Takano was her Fitzwilliam Darcy, until he broke her heart when she was seventeen and he was eighteen by running away during a school trip.

At that time, it was all that everyone could talk about. It had happened during a theater trip to Corpus Christi, Texas. Koji sneaked out of his room and left the hotel. The cameras of the hotel showed him walking out of the hotel, but never coming back. He had left his luggage in the hotel room, and all the boys that shared his room claimed that Koji didn't know he was planning to run away. When they questioned Belinda, Koji's girlfriend at the time, she made it clear to them that Koji hadn't run away. They had planned their future that same night, and he didn't indicate that he was unhappy in anyway. She plead with everyone that something else had happened to him, but the investigator came up empty handed. Koji was declared a runaway, and it was easier for her to believe that he was another runaway than that he was a victim of foul play.

Her world dimmed that day, but her life continued. She had gone to college to study to be a lawyer but quit to work in a theater, a place where she had fond memories. Her daily theater life never lived up to the days when she would hide with Koji behind the curtains. He often hid behind the curtains waiting for her and would grab her wrist and pull her to him and plant a kiss on her lips. Years after his mysterious disappearance, she still expected him to grab her by the wrist when she walked by a curtain.

Belinda spent the day drinking vodka and reliving her life with Koji. Each memory caused her smile to widen, making her unrecognizable to herself. She had tried smiling after Koji, but his memory never let her rest in peace. It seemed unfair to move away from her first love.

Her alarm announced it was time to go to work and she forced herself out the door and into a cab. New York City was her temporary home before she had to go to Mexico, and then move to Japan. After she fulfilled her Japan contact, she was at the wind's mercy. She had become a fan of running away, and never had the courage to grow roots to any of the cities she moved to.

She could still feel the alcohol fogging her senses but did her best to set the props before the company met up for notes. She wanted to finish the task before the new college students showed up to shadow the company.

"Belinda," she heard the stage manager call her name.

"What's up, Roger?" she turned to face two familiar faces, Roger and a face she hadn't seen in years. He was just as she remembered him, his mesmerizing almond eyes, and the bump on his nose where he broke it during a soccer match and his grin curved to the side in a way it made her swoon as a teenager.

"This is Ryu. This is the student that will be shadowing you for a few days," Roger informed her before turning to the ghost of Koji. "Belinda is one of our most responsible members. Just follow her example and you will succeed in the theatre world. I'll leave you guys to set up."

Roger left them without saying another word. Both stood in place staring at each other.

Even though Roger had introduced him as Ryu, Belinda was convinced that she was staring at Koji, or the alcohol was causing her to have delusions. It was impossible for her to mistake the face she had once loved; after all, he didn't share the wrinkles that marked her face or the silver hair that grew out in her late 20s. Koji's face was frozen in time, but he was as she remembered him that night that he promised to marry her after college. Neither of them moved until she finally let out a whisper, "Koji?"

His smile exposed long sharp canine teeth as he grabbed her by the wrist and pulled her unto the curtain.

Divorce Season

It was divorce season – four months out of the year where Noelle Hernández was drowning in new divorce filings, and she wasn't ready to go back to the files on her desk. Noelle was a legal assistant for a local attorney. That morning, she wasn't in the mood to face the broken-hearted victims of divorce season, and she was unaware that she was about to become one.

There was a knock at the door that interrupted her morning routine. She looked up at the only digital clock still connected in her house – 7:24 a.m. Besides her sister, no one came to visit her early, and she had never been one to knock.

She opened the door to discover a well-dressed man with papers in his hand.

"Noelle Hernández?" he asked.

"That's me," she answered. "How can I help you?"

He held the papers up for her and she reached for them. "I need your signature on the second page."

"I'm sorry but I'm not going to sign anything." Her legal assistant instincts came out in the form of an attitude.

"It's a citation and an Original Petition for Divorce," he explained. "You need to sign for the papers. You will have 20 days . . . ."

She moved her hand up to interrupt him. "You have the wrong person. I'm not married."

"Is your name Noelle Hernández?"

"Yes," she answered.

"I have the right address, and you're the one in the photo," he said as he handed her a cell phone. "If you are trying to avoid getting served, I'm not going to fall for it."

She looked at the phone and it was her face looking back at her. She was smiling, with a ring on her left ring finger, next to a handsome man whom she didn't recognize. The man in the suit reached for his phone, and hesitantly she gave him his possession.

"Well, I'm not going to sign a document meant for another person," she said in a daze, still trying to place the man in the photo and the unknown background behind them. She had never been married, and hadn't been interested in dating since starting her position at the law office.

"If you have any questions you can contact the attorney," the man instructed her. "His information is on the last page."

Noelle ignored him and walked back into her home to look for the attorney's signature block on the last page. She saw the name of the attorney, and she immediately recognized the name, Xande Lichtenstein. She let out a sigh of relief. The attorney who prepared and executed the original petition was notorious in her office for his mistakes. A number of his clients had fired him and hired her boss.

214

On the drive to Attorney Lichtenstein's office, she called her work office to ask for permission to be late to take care of the misunderstanding. It could be easily taken care of over the phone, but there she was waiting in the lobby of Attorney Lichtenstein's office. Noelle certainly didn't have any obligation to her namesake who has going to get served with divorce papers, but it was unmistakably her in that photo. A quick search on her phone's gallery and Facebook's album left her empty-handed, no similar picture to the one the process server had.

The staff seemed busy trying to keep up with divorce season, and it was going to be some time before she could speak with a legal assistant. She curiously read the petition. The man divorcing Noelle Hernández was Paul Cooney. Their marriage had taken place about three years ago in Las Vegas. Another coincidence she shared with her namesake, she had never been a fan of traditional weddings, and her ideal wedding included a trip to Las Vegas. According to the document, they didn't have children. The reason for the divorce was cited as "insupportable." She wondered how their marriage had become insupportable.

Yelling from down the hall forced her to look up to a disgruntled client, but was surprised to be facing the man who was divorcing Noelle Hernández, Paul Cooney

"Noelle." His voice sent shivers down her spine. "Did you get served with the divorce paper?" he asked.

"Yes, I have them right here." Having been caught reading a sensitive document, she stumbled to rise from her seat and hand him his paper. "The process server made a mistake and gave them to me instead of your soon to be ex-wife."

"Come on!" His sudden burst startled her. "Don't you start, too? This morning is weird enough without you going along with their madness." He grabbed her by the wrist. "Come on. We are going to clear this up."

She wanted to swat his hand, but she was curious to find out how he knew Noelle. They went into a conference room where two women were on their laptops. He pushed the petition into the hands of the closest female to him.

"This is the petition that your office prepared, and this is my wife who got served this morning. How is it that you can't find my name in your open client list?" he yelled at them.

Noelle pulled her arm out of his gasp. "I'm sorry, but I'm not your wife."

"You know what I mean," he looked back at her.

"No, I don't know what you mean. I don't know you," she told him, then looked around him to the females, "And, I'm only here to tell the attorney that I'm not the Noelle on the petition. I've said what I came to say, and I need to go to work." Without waiting for a response, she turned around and made her way to the entrance. Paul followed her out into the hallway. He reached for her as her hand touched the handle on the door.

"Noelle, wait."

She turned to look at him. He was just her type, and that made her weak in the knees.

He continued, "I don't understand what is going on with the world today. The legal secretaries can't find me in their system, and now you are claiming that we aren't married. Who did I marry then?"

"I'm the one who's confused. I've never been married. So, it is impossible for me to be getting a divorce."

"If I didn't marry you, then who is in all of these pictures," he said, handing her his phone opened to his gallery app.

It was Noelle and Paul in front of a decorated Christmas tree; it was them on a beach, in a park, and in a room she had never been in, and it was a gallery of a life she never lived. She couldn't find an explanation.

"Look maybe there's a reason why they lost my file; maybe we can still fix us." He didn't wait for her to speak. "Let's go to Haiku Café and have a *matcha latte*. We can talk about us."

That was her favorite café and her drink of choice. She was still holding onto his phone when Paul playfully pushed her toward the door and opened the door for her. She walked out, and felt the phone slipping from her hands.

She scanned the ground, but couldn't find it. She looked back to find that Paul hadn't followed her outside. Noelle went into the law office, but Paul wasn't in the lobby. She made her way to the conference room to find both females on their feet searching for something. One looked up her way.

"Excuse me, Mrs. Cooney," one of the legal secretaries addressed her. "Did Mr. Cooney take the petition with him?"

Noelle shook her head no.

"Thank you. We'll find it. It has to be around here."

The paper had disappeared along with the phone and Paul. Noelle turned around and made her way to her vehicle.

She sat alone in her car looking for her cell phone in her purse. She pressed on her Facebook app and typed his name in the search bar. His handsome face was the second option on the results. She clicked on his name to learn more about him. Paul's Facebook profile had him as single. He worked at a dentist's office five blocks away from her work office, and had checked in having breakfast in Cancun that morning. He was currently miles away, and she wondered who she had talked to a few minutes ago. She moved the screen up, and clicked on the "Friend Request" icon.

A Love Letter to the Monkees

Camilla's finger felt heavy lingering over the touch pad, the pointer on the screen over the buy icon. She considered if she should buy, or jump back in time, for the signed wool hat by Mike Nesmith, a member of The Monkees, her favorite retro band. Camilla was introduced to the band's show during a channel surfing binge. In her awkward life, she was captivated by the idea of "four insane boys" and their surreal TV lives. She considered herself their number one fan, and her mishaps were proof of her love for the talented artists.

The wool hat had been on her wish list and watch list on EBay for quite a while. She wanted a piece of history from a generation that brightened the world with their voices and music. She didn't mind paying $299 for the wool hat, but the lack of authenticity made her rethink her purchase. That is where her incredible gift came in – time travel – an unexplainable and hard to control ability which she discovered around the same time she saw the first episode.

She still hadn't forgiven herself for destroying the world after a jump to the set of The Monkees' show while they were filming "Monkee See, Monkee

Die." The 2018 world that Camilla originally came from was a different place. The earth was greener, and climate change wasn't a hot topic. The values of society were different than what she had known in her former life. Hover boards were energized by the sun, and the world's biggest problem was the garbage deficiency for fueling and heating. But, when she went back in time, she didn't consider how a short romance with a Monkee would affect the world she knew. Now, society was stuck with Millennials glued to electric devices and without their self-adjusting shoes.

She had gone back many times to fix the damage she had caused, but each time she caused a bigger devastation. She settled in the most tolerable reality. She had adjusted to living under the Rio Grande Valley sun, and The Monkees were still a renowned band. Also, it beat living in a time line where children were forced to fight each other. Staring at the screen, she had convinced herself that she had always been too ambitious with her souvenirs and that no one would miss a wool hat from the '60s.

The Shadow Brother

I'm not an attention seeker, and I am confident that everything that I am about to share happened in Nuevo Laredo, Mexico, in October 2012. I didn't dream it. Years later, I still can't tell this story in its full context. I'm going to change names, relationships, and try to be as vague as possible without it affecting the story telling. I am not dramatizing. This is how I remember that summer morning.

In August 2012, I had an unexplained urge to travel to Mexico. It was a nagging feeling to quit my life and travel around Mexico collecting stories and work on my dream of being a writer. I listened to my instinct and quit my job. I packed my car and drove to Nuevo Laredo with the Mexican Drug War raging on in the background.

My timing has never been on point, and I was in Nuevo Laredo during the Mexican Drug Wars, a war between the Mexican military and various cartels for territory and use of the borders. During my stay, I learned that Nuevo Laredo's bridge sees 40% export usage into the United States. It meant I woke up to frequent shootings and screams from the neighbor-hood. Once I woke up because the earth moved with a loud boom overshadowed by car alarms and scared dog barks. It became a habit for me to add to my nightly prayers, "Dear God, please don't let me hear anything or see anything while I sleep. Amen."

I'll skip all the boring details of how I filled my day and go straight to a hot night in October 2012. Let me set it up. I had already stayed in Mexico for a month and a half. I was staying at a cozy and unique three-floor home. My room was on the first floor connected to the main house with an open hallway that ended at the courtyard. The unique design allowed my room to have a window that opened out into the hallway, a small window on the door, and three long, rectangular slit-windows facing to the neighbor's backyard. I was told by the owner that it was designed so that a stray bullet couldn't hit any of the bedrooms.

The house always had guests, carpenters, and work staff come and go. For some odd reason, only three people stayed the night. I was running late to meet my ride to Saltillo, Mexico, which I missed. Maria, the housekeeper, left on time, leaving me locked outside of the house and waiting for someone to open up for me. Julia, the owner of the house and mother of Javier, a teenage boy, were the only ones that showed up.

The night was hot, and my room didn't have air conditioning. I opened all of the rectangular slit windows at the top of the room, two windows facing the hallway to the courtyard, and the small window on the door. It wasn't enough and I kept drinking water to cool down. The heat kept me up, and I decided to change into shorts to cool down. As I reached my drawer, a voice within my head said, "No, what if they kidnap you?" My instincts had never been a loud and clear voice before, and I decided to listen to the voice out of fear, and I stayed in my yoga pants to go to bed. I closed all of the windows facing into the hallway before I got into my bed. When I finally feel asleep, I found myself in an odd location.

I was walking on a set of an old western, and I noticed a cowboy with a gold star pinned on his chest. He looked past me and pointed without even giving me a glance and said, "It will be over soon. *Quince.*" I turned to the direction he was pointing and saw a dust cloud blowing my way with ghastly roar with sounds of a female yell. When the dust reached me, I woke up to excited dogs barking. I assumed a bomb had been detonated and that is what had frightened the animals.

The animals and I soon started to calm down, and all of the water I had drunk hours before was really bothering me. I decided to get up to use the restroom when, in my groggy state, I heard the voice again within my head say, "No, they will hear you." A normal person might have dismissed the voice as their imagination, but I was half asleep and asked, "Who?"

"I don't know, but they will hear you if you move."

I stayed still and listened for unknown footsteps, but only heard the fan. I asked the voice, "Do I turn off the fan?"

"No, they might hear the bed move," the voice answered. I waited, but my needs became stronger and as I twitched my muscles to move, a shadow stopped me. I had a sense of familiarity, and the shadow walked by the windows to the courtyard. I felt immediate relief. I was sure that it was Javier walking towards his room to get ready for school. I stirred in the bed to move out of bed.

"Not yet. Wait until in comes back." The voice advised.

I understood. I hadn't heard footsteps following the shadow, and no sounds of rummage in the next door bedroom. (As I'm writing this, I realized that the shadow was impossible to be made by a human. The only light at the time was the moon and a dim light from the living room.)

Without a clock, and my cell phone out of reach, I don't know how long I waited in the dark for the shadow to walk past my window, but it never walked past my bedroom.

My alarming need forced me to speak up, "I need to get up."

"Okay, but quietly open the window and peek out to see if they are gone." The voice in my head said.

"Who?"

"I don't know," the voice whispered.

I quietly rolled out of my bed and tip-toed to the door. I pressed my hand on the window to minimize the vibration and sound. I slowly moved the handle on the window. Once I succeeded in opening the

224

window, I looked to the side to the empty hall and only saw light bouncing off the walls from the living room. I cautiously opened the door and walked out of my room listening for "them." When I reached the living room, I saw Julia sitting on the sofa with the phone pressed to her ear. With relief, I greeted her and ran to the guest bathroom. Before I closed the door, I got to overhear her say, "They kidnapped Javier."

While I was sleeping, three men, claiming to be part of the Mexican cartel, waited outside the house for an opportunity to break into the gated house. When Julia opened the door to the street, they ran at her with guns. They shoved her to the ground and yelled commands. When Javier walked into the scene, Julia yelled at him to run, and he tried his best to run to the second floor before one of the men caught up with him and took him next to Julia. I will always be grateful to them because when they were asked if anyone else was in the house, they both lied and said it was just them.

It is unbelievable that I slept through all of the commotion, but I didn't hear any of it just as I had prayed that night. It might have been the fan that drowned some of the noise, but I think the hum of the fan was too soft to be heard outside my door. I think it has something to do with my prayer not to see anything or hear anything. It would explain the voice in my head that calmly guided me and that shadow that stopped me from walking out.

It hasn't been the first time a shadow of a man has appeared to help me when I'm in need of assistance. In a fall morning of 2008, I woke up in my room fully aware that an intruder was in my room. Without a second thought, I threw my bed sheet to use as a shield to hide where I was running. But I got a clear glance of a man's silhouette standing in front of the internet router light. As I reached the light by the door, I heard a loud bang on the floor. When the light came on, I was standing in my bedroom alone with a book in the middle of the empty floor. I took the book and found a document I had misplaced. Somehow, the book had flown off my bookcase to the middle of the room.

I have theories about that night and the identity of the shadow. Theory one is that the shadow is that of my older brother who, unfortunately, was miscarried four years before I was born. There are hours of therapy records of me talking about a brother who I missed but I never met. In my mind, growing up would have been easier if I had my big brother next to me. It would explain why I felt a certain familiarity and peace when the shadow walked past my bedroom.

Theory number two is that it was one of my seven brothers, a Bali belief. I recently read "Eat, Pray, Love" by Elizabeth Gilbert. There's a scene where Ms. Gilbert explains to Ketut Liyer, her advisor in Indonesia, that a man with a knife stands over her as she sleeps but is gone when she fully awakens. Ketut Liyer shares a Bali belief in which each person has seven brothers protecting them. These brothers can only be seen when we are in a groggy state. He explained to Ms. Gilbert that it is her brother she is seeing when she is waking up. I tried researching his idea, but have been unsuccessful. Both times that I have seen the shadow is when I need help, I'm waking up and still groggy, and when my dogs are not with me.

I believe the dream was getting me ready for the upcoming 48 hours. In a way I was conscience of the noises outside of the bedroom that morning. I must have heard them, and my subconscious created a surreal movie set for me to walk into. I have often wondered why the cowboy said *quince*, fifteen in Spanish. During the negotiation process, I thought the cowboy had giving me the number of hours that we were going to be without Javier, but it took 36-48 hours for the kidnappers to let him go. To this day, I believe I'm overlooking something that my subconscious noticed.

I'm going to skip a lot of the details of the rescue. That story belongs to Javier, not to me. I was in lock-down in my room until the morning after Javier was returned safely. There were no arrests made, and we were all left with our own theory of the identity of the kidnappers. But I will share this last thing.

During the time negotiations were happening, I learned why I needed to be present that morning. I missed my ride to Saltillo. I hadn't planned on being there that morning, and all of the work staff had this information. But the spiritual world needed me to let go of the past and stop fighting a war that had never been mine to fight. I'm going to leave with that curiosity in mind. Maybe one day I will share about a feud that started before I was born, but that's not my story.

$\mathcal{A}$rnaldo "J. R." $\mathcal{R}$amirez III

Born in McAllen, Texas, J. R. is the only boy of four siblings. His sisters are Dalinda, Melissa, and Clarissa. J. R.'s full name is Arnaldo Ramirez III. His father is Arnaldo "Nano" Ramirez Jr. His mother Dalinda Ramirez is a school teacher in McAllen. She formerly taught at the elementary school where J. R. went, met, and made friends who he still has to this day. J. R. graduated from McAllen Memorial High School and earned a Marketing Degree in the College of Business from Texas Tech University.

After college, J. R. worked for his father in various businesses, but focused on a career in the music industry. He worked at his father's La Villa Real Convention Center. J. R. founded the first electronic ticketing company in the Rio Grande Valley, RGV TICKETING. With their experience and knowledge of the music industry, J. R. helped his father design the Pharr Events Center. J. R. was the initial general manager for two years before being stricken with multiple sclerosis in 2012.

J. R. has moved on since the onset of his disability. Now his sense of purpose is writing. He has a passion for writing memoirs and poetry, as reflected in his work in this anthology. Music is in his blood. According to J. R., "Music is poetry and things could be worse. When one door closes, another door opens, so I write."

J. R.'s great uncle Rafael Ramirez was a famous international music composer. He wrote "Llorrarás," a song that was played at many weddings. His great uncle played Cupid by introducing J. R.'s mom to his dad at the family's Falcon Recording Studio. Arnaldo Ramirez Sr., J. R.'s grandfather, was the founder of the Falcon Recording Studio. Also known as "Mr. Falcon," he recorded and distributed hundred of records. Before opening the legendary La Villa Real, J. R.'s father "Nano" was the producer at the studio and ran the corporation.

J. R believes, "Music is therapy for the soul."

Meditate

I meditate to clear my mind;
nobody knows what I go through now.
But somehow I persevere because deep in my heart
I think about all the support
and love I receive – all geared toward me.
That is fantastic! Am I being dramatic?
Maybe. So I'll try to be strong –
and manly –
Until a cure for MS comes along –
eventually.
I know people are concerned,
but through trial and error I have learned
what I can and should not do.
You will notice, too.
And it needs to be said I know what is in store.
I've "been to that rodeo" before.
I know what I'm doing –
I hope.

Water Rescue

Let me tell you a story. Yes, this really happened. I was headed to the town of Port Mansfield, Texas, on Friday, March 26th. The night before, I had had a full night's sleep. I would not have another one until on April 1st, April Fool's Day. The date never dawned on me, and when I told my friends what had happened, they thought it was an April Fool's joke. *But this was no joke.*

And so the story begins. I was so-o-o-o excited to be going fishing in Port Mansfield, where I had heard stories of people catching big fish! I could not wait. We were going to my friend Chase Smith's fishing shack. A shack is a cabin for fishing in the middle of the water accessible only by boat. His shack was about an hour north of Port Mansfield, and we got off to a late start. It was dark when we departed. I couldn't leave before sunset, so my friend towed my boat for me, and I joined everyone there at Port Mansfield. There were two boats with five people on my boat which was a 17-foot Bay Master with an 88-horse-power engine. On Chase's boat were four people and a dog. I didn't have enough life jackets for five people on my boat, and the Coast Guard was not going to let me leave until I went to buy three more life jackets at Wal-Mart in the town of Raymondville, about 30 minutes away.

A cold front, or northern, was approaching. It was very windy out of the south which was feeding the cold front. All the compartments on my boat were full with equipment, and I didn't know where to put the lifejackets, so we decided to put them on. Everyone on the other boat was laughing at us. Oh, well—it was a good thing we did!

The cold front was supposed to arrive at 2 am. The Coast Guard had told us not to mess around and to tie up as soon as we had arrived at the shack. We were almost there. It was the calm before the storm. It was absolutely so still that you could use a lighter. I should have known that was not good. Suddenly, the cold wind punched me in the face. The rain was coming down so hard that it hurt and a wave was coming. There was nothing I could do. The wave came in and instantly went through my boat, filling it up with water. Another one was coming; I thought, *if that wave comes, it is going to sink my boat. So turn the boat around and go with the waves back to Port Mansfield.* Well, I did not make the turn around. The wave came upon us, flipped and capsized my boat, throwing all of us into the water. Fortunately, Chase made the turn.

Chase and his group headed east straight for land before his radio shorted out. We were about 45 minutes north of Port Mansfield in the middle of the Inter Coastal Waterway. Chase's group was able to call *MAYDAY*. The Coast Guard answered their call, found them on land via helicopter, dropped them a radio, and Chase told them there was another boat –

mine.   I had a spotlight, and turned it on for a moment. Thank God.   The people on Chase's boat saw the spotlight go way up, then down, then nothing. We were in the middle of a wave, so they thought the worst

That same night, my mom had a flight. Luckily she departed before the storm and made it to Dallas safely; however she had a gut feeling something was wrong and spoke with my dad upon arriving. Funny thing, a mother's instinct. My dad didn't know anything was wrong.

Okay, I thought to myself and said as I pointed east, "If the boat sinks, swim that way and eventually you'll be able to stand." Through the lighting you could catch a glimpse of a tree line and land, but we were quite far away – about three miles. So I instructed everyone to take their shoes off so they would be able to swim better. I could hear a helicopter that was looking for us, but they couldn't see us through the clouds and rain. After a while the rain started letting up. Eventually the clouds went away, but we didn't hear or see the helicopter. The helicopter had gone back to refuel at their station in Corpus Christi. This was the only time in my life I voluntarily had put on a life jacket. Next thing I know, I'm in the water wearing it.

All of us were able to hold onto the boat while we waited. I felt bad for the two guys I didn't know, but we were all in this together. The fact that this happened at night didn't help. It was cold. We were wet and a north wind was blowing, so it actually felt warmer underneath the water. Things began to get dire. About five hours had gone by; my friend took off his life jacket and said "Save yourselves."

We got mad saying, "No! No! No! Come on man. Hold it together." Then we finally heard, and then saw the helicopter looking for us. They found us. A diver jumped into the water and he raised us to the helicopter. I was the last one to go up – captain of the ship pride.

I was proud of the guys for bonding together and getting through the ordeal. Initially, I thought I was going to be in some kind of trouble for breaking some mariner law. The Coast Guard said, "No. We are glad you guys are alright, and this is what we do." They flew us to a Naval station in Corpus Christi and we waited for Chase to pick us up. While we waited, the Coast Guard showed me with the wind, current, etc., where my boat should be. More on my boat in a moment.

Chase told me that that the Coast Guard had taken them back to Port Mansfield. I guess the town was apprised by radio of the situation, because when Chase's group arrived back to Port Mansfield, townsfolk were waiting for them with towels and blankets. What good folks. It was such a beautiful day at sunrise the next morning – the calm after the storm

After Chase picked my group up in Corpus Christi, we went back to Port Mansfield and checked into a hotel. I was still pumping adrenaline and couldn't sleep while we waited for a friend of ours to show up with his boat, so we could look for mine. Three hours later he showed up and we went forth. He had an off-shore boat, so we had to travel down the inter-costal water way. After a while, we saw a boat being towed into port. It was my boat. We yelled at the guys towing the boat, wanting them to stop. They ignored us; they were trying to steal my boat. So we chased them back to port. As we got closer to port, I leaped from the off-shore boat and jumped on to mine. That was a stupid thing to do. I could have slipped and gotten hurt, but I didn't. That was my boat and all our equipment and bags were on it. Since I made the jump safely, the boat thieves had to tow me in. Before getting into a confrontation with the thieves, we called the sheriff. The sheriff found wallets in the bags, realized it was our stuff, and gave us permission to get it. To hell with those guys. Things were getting ugly with them. If it hadn't been for the sheriff, a confrontation surely would have happened. With everything that we went through, that was the last thing we needed. I wanted to get into a fight and break something; that's why I jumped onto my boat. Everybody's equipment and bags were returned except mine. My bag was missing and my keys and wallet were in my bag.

So after all that, Chase and I drove back to McAllen an hour away to get my spare keys, then returned to Port Mansfield to get my boat, and towed it back. What a mess. Then we returned to Chase's house in McAllen. Still pumping with adrenaline, we couldn't sleep, so we watched a movie his mom had rented; it was "White Squall," and quite appropriate. It's a movie about a boat that gets caught in a storm. The next day was April Fool's Day and I got my first full night's rest in three days.

***

Anyway, a month or so later, I got a package from a rural carrier. We didn't have a physical address, so I wrote 6 ¼ Mile Line on my address line on my driver's license. My license, of course, was in my wallet which I lost with my bag. *Odd*, I thought, *who knows I live in a rural area?* Well, the package was for me. It was my wallet and my keys. I wanted to send a thank-you card, but there was no return address. And the sixty dollars I had had in my wallet were still there – three $20 bills.

Steven Ramírez

Steven Ramírez was born October 6, 1951 in Edinburg, Texas, and is a long-time Valley resident. He began an early love of reading at age three. Seeing an advertisement for a popular beer in a newspaper, he shocked his parents by pointing to the ad and saying the word JAX. This led to a three-year junior consultancy as the subject for reading experiments with his father Al Ramírez, at Pan American College in his initial search for best methods in early bilingual education.

After attending Sam Houston Elementary, Ramírez next went to Edinburg Junior High and began polishing his writing skills by competing in UIL Ready Writing contests. Entering Edinburg High School in the fall of 1967, he worked on the school newspaper all four years, first as a reporter/photographer, then as an assignment editor, and finally as newspaper editor his junior and senior years. He and a family friend worked after school delivering the Edinburg Daily Review and the McAllen Evening Monitor newspapers to convenience store chains and businesses from Mission to Mercedes.

Steven continued in newspaper work at Pan American University in 1972, writing articles, editorials and features for El Bronco and working on a liberal arts degree. Several years later, he abandoned a BA in English to pursue a Business Administration degree in sales and marketing.

In early 1976, he met and married the lovely and talented Valerie Goerlitz and soon had three gifted and talented daughters. He decided to turn sales and marketing knowledge into reality and, in 1983, the family moved to Brownsville where Ramírez began work selling industrial equipment to the largest maquiladora plants in Matamoros and Reynosa. This was before NAFTA, when major product representatives didn't know twin plants existed across the border in Deep South Texas. Later he worked for a commercial printing company and a retail book franchise. He recently created an indie publishing company, Omni-Media Publishing.

Steven's writing interests are historical fiction and crime and mystery. He is currently working on an historical family saga.

Ninety Minutes
With the Champ

In mid-July, 1970, I was in New York City staying with friends, all students at Fordham University in the Bronx. Friends were urging me to enroll in undergraduate classes at Fordham that coming fall. I was considering the idea, despite already low-fifties overnight temperatures, something I would quickly have to get used to. Then, on July 24, came a call from home in deep south Texas: an order to appear on August 3rd before my local draft board in McAllen, Texas, for a "status review." Deciding to stay, I called the Selective Service office in McAllen and asked for a location transfer so I could appear before a New York City draft board. "I'm sorry, sir," a secretary explained, "but we cannot change the review location. The McAllen office retains original jurisdiction."

Pressed for time, with only eight days to travel 2,000 miles back home, I searched for an express bus schedule to meet my needs but could not find one. A Fordham student from Atlanta suggested checking with the Southern Pacific Railway, so I called for student fare information.

A ticket agent explained, "We have passenger service on the *Southern Crescent* from Washington,

D. C. through Atlanta to New Orleans, with a connection to San Antonio on the *Sunset Limited*, Southern Pacific's long-haul passenger train."

"When would I arrive in San Antonio?" I asked, worried about the timing.

"The *Sunset Limited* departs New Orleans at 10:15 p.m. the evening of July, 30th and arrives in San Antonio the next morning, Friday, July, 31st, at 7 a.m. The one-way student rail pass fare is $150. Purchase the student pass early this coming Monday morning at Penn Station and take the 8:15 a.m. express commuter train to Washington, D. C. to make your connection."

***

At 7:45 a.m. the following Monday, July 27, I ran double-time into Penn Station in mid-town Manhattan to purchase the rail pass and crossed into a world of chaos. Lost in the middle of rush hour in New York City's main inter-regional rail hub, I was swept along with tens of thousands of commuters coming at me from every direction, all seeming to know exactly where they were going. Confused, I moved with the crowd, but with no idea how to find the Penn Central ticket window. Eventually reaching the center of the massive concourse, I stopped to ask people rushing past for help. No one paid any attention.

Seeing me stranded in the middle of the concourse, a kind porter took pity and accompanied me to the correct ticket window. Joining a slow-moving queue to purchase my ticket, I calmed a little and began silently praying for divine intervention that I might truthfully enjoy the odyssey facing me, crossing half the continent on my way back home. Still, the uncertainty of what awaited me at my appointment with the Selective Service board clouded my mind.

When I got to the ticket window, the Penn Central agent coldly broke through my troubled concentration. "Ticket to where?" he barked in a loud voice.

"I need a student rail pass for the *Southern Crescent* with connection to San Antonio, Texas." I waited for a total.

"We discontinued pass-throughs for the Southern Railway on July 1st," the agent said. "You can purchase the pass at Union Station in D. C. That'll be $20 for the D. C. ticket." Taking my cash, he handed me my ticket and said, "Your train is at Platform 6."

"Where is that?" I asked, looking around the cavernous building.

The agent pointed to the nearby hallway entrance for Platforms 6 through 11. "It's over *that* way," he said, obviously annoyed, and then added, "You had better hurry, too. They announced the final boarding call over five minutes ago."

Quickly running through the hallway entrance, I started down a wide set of one-way stairs descending into semi-darkness. In panic mode, trotting faster and faster without seeing signs directing me, I began running hard, fighting the creeping feeling I was going to miss my train. At last, I saw a well-lit sign with a red arrow pointing to Platform 6. Sprinting at full speed, I got to the platform and saw the train moving quickly away. Without breaking stride, I jumped and landed on the bottom step of the last car.

Entering through the car doorway and walking up the aisle, all I saw was wall-to-wall passengers. I counted twenty-eight rows of seats, with two seats on either side. All fifty-six seats were taken. It was the same in the second and third cars; all seats occupied. Walking out the third car door, I stood for a moment on a platform between the cars. As we entered a tunnel under the Hudson River, I opened the door of the fourth car and stepped inside.

My immediate reaction was one of mild shock; not only was the car empty, it was nothing like the others. Instead of double rows of double seats, it had two long plastic platform seats running the entire length of the car. The seats faced each other, with a wide aisle between them, like in a subway car, but without breaks in the seats where the subway doors would be.

Looking once again to the other end of the car, I saw it was not empty. On the left side, at the far end, a black gentleman sat comfortably balancing an open briefcase on his lap. Slowly stepping forward, I saw he had a phone receiver in his hand, its coiled wire stretching down into the briefcase. I stood and watched him nodding emphatically, and then speak forcefully for a time before disconnecting and beginning another conversation. He did this several times. The ambient sounds of the accelerating train made it impossible to hear anything he was saying.

As he continued his conversations, I moved even closer and realized this was a large and *very* well-dressed gentleman. Studying his expertly-tailored charcoal grey suit, a vibrant red tie, and black wingtip shoes, my analytical skills went into overdrive. With all the attributes of a very important person – confident, obviously successful, positively in control – he must be a high-powered entrepreneur I figured. Watching him work his mobile phone, only then did it occur to me – he had requested seating in this car so he could quietly take care of business without any interruption. Turning away, I started to walk to the other end of the car.

Suddenly, the gentleman said, "Wait up. Come back and join me."

Turning back, I saw he had put the phone in the briefcase and put it aside, so I started down to his end of the car. Once there, I did a double-take, this time in very real shock. The gentleman sitting in front of me was the recently reigning world heavyweight champion of boxing, Muhammad Ali.

Wide-eyed, I shouted, "Is it really you, Champ, live and in color?"

"Yes, it is, but don't tell everybody," he said with a smile. "I'm in disguise."

"Amen to *that!*" I said, complimenting his excellent camouflage. "The briefcase phone and your polished style captured my attention and held it.

Thinking you were a VIP businessman, I didn't want to intrude."

"That's the general idea," he said. "Most everyone has only seen me in pictures and on television, almost always in boxing gear, and never dressed like this. Even up close, people focus on the disguise. They usually leave me alone."

At that moment, a conductor came through the door at our end of the car and announced Newark was the next stop. After taking and perforating our tickets, he handed the tickets back, but then took the time to slowly look Ali up and down. Shaking his head, he said, "You know, you look just like Muhammad Ali."

"Yeah," Ali said with a relaxed grin, "I get that all the time."

"My mistake," the conductor said, walking away and shaking his head.

Ali turned to me. "Live and in color, huh?" he said with a quick laugh. "I'm headed to Philadelphia. How about you?"

"I'm on my way back home to Texas," I said with a long sigh.

"Sounds like you're not looking forward to the trip. What's going on in Texas?"

Not wanting to burden him with my problems, I looked away, uncertain how to answer. Something prompted me to tell him anyway. "I have a date with my draft board on the 3rd for a status review."

"Really?" His interest was quick and totally unexpected. "What did they tell you?"

"Nothing at all," I said. "I got a phone call about a form letter addressed to me saying to show up on the 3rd for this review. That was it. I have no idea what it means."

"Before this, has the draft board communicated with you in any way?" Ali said.

"No," I shook my head, "not since I registered over nine months ago."

"Let me tell you, that's a very good sign," he said. "Can I help you figure this out?"

"Please," I beamed. "I would appreciate any help you could give me."

"First, tell me what you did when you first registered," he said.

"I did what I felt was morally and ethically correct," I said. "I filed as a conscientious objector (CO), with a 1-O classification, 'available for civilian work contributing to the national health, safety, or interest.'" I looked down at the floor. "My greatest fear is my request will be denied, and I'll be classified 1-A."

"Put that worry aside," he smiled. "At this point in time, there is very little chance that will happen. The reason? Fewer than 5% of eligible draftees file for conscientious objector status when they register. Draft boards put those CO claims aside simply because their main job is managing the other 95%. That's why you're just now hearing from them."

Ali then explained the structure of a "status review," and what I might expect in the way of questions designed to disqualify my CO request.

"At first," he said, "they'll ask loaded questions like, 'Why are you opposed to the Vietnam war?' You need to be honest and sincere and say you're opposed to participating in any war. Tell them it's not a political or philosophical view, or an objection to any given policy. It's your deeply held religious belief."

"Excellent answers," I said smiling.

"Then they'll ask: 'Do you believe war is wrong?' Again, be honest and sincere and say you believe there can be legitimate reasons for our country going to war, but you simply object to personally participating in the armed conflict."

Shifting his focus, Ali raised his eyebrows and said, "Are you aware what the 1-O classification involves?"

"Not really," I said, shaking my head. "I have never seen any in-depth information about what 'civilian work' means, or what it would require."

"'Civilian work' means it has nothing to do with the military," he said. "You'll be available to do whatever educational, social and/or community service your local draft board may want."

"Is that something new?" I said, suddenly enthused. "How is it *you* know about it?"

"Well, let me tell you," he nodded, frustration clearly showing in his face. "I know because I learned about it the hard way in my own case." He did not react in anger, but I could see it in his eyes.

I quickly said, "I don't know anything but what I've heard and read about your case. Tell me if this much is correct: Based on your religious belief as a

Muslim, you refused to join the U. S. Army when ordered to enlist. In refusing, you committed felony draft evasion, punishable on conviction by five years in prison and a $10,000 fine. The criminal offense prompted the World Boxing Association to suspend your boxing license, and the New York Athletic Commission to strip you of your championship title. Is this right so far?"

"Basically, yes," he said. "but my boxing license and title were taken away before I was officially charged with anything. That's just one more deceitful *technicality*."

"Then, let me say this," I said. "Your refusal to enlist, and your supposed lack of patriotism have never mattered one bit to me. People are saying every negative thing about you because they can't or won't accept your standing up for your beliefs. What I'd like to know is the reason for your initial defiance of the draft law. I've never read or heard it explained."

"It has never been reported accurately," he said. "I registered for the draft in Louisville, Kentucky in 1960. In 1964, at age 22, I failed my pre-induction physical because my reading skills didn't meet the U. S. Army's acceptable standards. The draft board classified me 1-Y, qualified for military service, but only in time of war or national emergency.

"By February of 1966," he continued, "the war in Vietnam was raging, with more than 400,000 troops already in country, and the Pentagon issued a call for an expanded draft. All draft boards were directed to reclassify any 1-Y persons 1-A, meaning immediately available for military service. The draft board failed to inform me of that change. When I found out, I filed for CO status, claiming exemption from military service based on my religious belief as a Muslim. The draft board rejected my claim. I appealed to the Kentucky State Appeal Board and they rejected my claim as well, without giving any reason for their decision.

"That eventually led to my conviction for draft evasion in federal district court in Texas," Ali said. "I immediately appealed to the U. S. Court of Appeals for the Fifth Circuit, which affirmed my conviction. I then asked the Supreme Court to review my case, but they refused and sent it back to the federal district court for review. After the lower court re-affirmed my conviction, I again appealed to the Fifth Circuit. Just last month, they upheld their original decision. Now, for the second time, I've asked the Supreme Court to review all lower court decisions for legal errors. That's where my case is today."

"What do you think are the chances of a favorable outcome?" I asked.

"I don't know about *Ali vs. the United States* at the Supreme Court. All I can do is wait and pray it goes my way. I do know this much," he said, quickly smiling, "I will box again soon."

"What's the deal?" I said.

"I'll tell you, but promise you won't say anything until you hear it on the news."

I raised my right hand and smiled. "I swear to keep it quiet, Champ."

"Since Georgia doesn't have a state boxing commission," he said with a grin, "the city of Atlanta is granting me a license to fight there. It's all legal. Nobody can stop it."

***

Too soon, the conductor came into the car and announced the next stop was Philadelphia's Penn Station. "This is where I leave," Ali said. "It's been my pleasure talking with you. I hope I've helped."

"You have, yes," I said. "Meeting you has been the best thing yet, a real honor. And you've totally improved my outlook on the coming status review. I can't thank you enough."

"You won't have any problem dealing with them." Ali stood and extended his hand.

When I shook it, his hand was twice as big as mine! I held up both fists just for fun.

Smiling, he bumped his fists with mine and then said, "*A Salaam Alaikum*. That's Arabic for, 'Peace be unto you.' You say, '*Wa Alaikum Salaam*' in return. It means, 'And unto you, peace.'"

I repeated it. "And unto you, peace, and success in your Supreme Court case."

"Thank you." With that he smiled, picked up his briefcase, and left the car.

***

Nine months later, Ali's sentence was overturned by a unanimous vote at the U. S. Supreme Court. The case set forth the standards a draftee must meet to qualify for conscientious objector status. Not surprisingly, they were the very things he told me

251

I needed to do. He had said, "Be honest and sincere, state one's opposition to participating in any war. Explaining one's stand is based on a deeply held religious belief."

Valerie Goerlitz Ramírez

Like the birth of twin boys three years earlier, Valerie's arrival in the evening of January 21, 1953, surprised her parents. Earlier in the day, the doctor had reassured her father that it was safe to go coach an out-of-town basketball game – no baby was coming that night. However, on his return, Mr. Goerlitz was met by his anxious sister telling him to quickly go to the hospital because Mary had delivered a baby girl.

Val's mother was delighted and had already named her Valerie with the middle name Ellen after Mary's grandmother. Although Valerie's dad really wanted another son – one of the twins had died shortly after birth – Valerie and her father spent a lot of time together going to the family garden and playing tennis. She was an avid fan of all her dad's various sports teams.

Goerlitz-Ramírez had a happy, small-town childhood and good school experiences in her hometown of Oakland City, Indiana. During high school, she participated in many activities including band, Spanish Club, and Hoosier Girls State at Indiana University in Bloomington. Later she became a student there and played on the women's tennis team.

Her junior year abroad was spent studying at La Católica in Lima, Perú and working at Colegio Roosevelt where she came in contact with the Baha'i faith which she later joined. Valerie also traveled through Bolivia, Brazil, Uruguay, and Argentina.

After returning to the United States in 1975, Ms. Goerlitz came to Texas to complete her student teaching in Mercedes at JFK Elementary. In 1976, she met and married Steven Ramírez. They have three daughters, and their family now includes two sons-in-law and a precious granddaughter born November 30, 2017.

Mrs. Ramírez began her teaching career at Donna Elementary in 1975 and also worked for Brownsville ISD and PSJA ISD before retiring from Edinburg CISD in 2009.

Goerlitz-Ramírez has enjoyed writing since high school and has composed many poems and written brief reflections during the busy years of working and raising a family. With the encouragement of The Write Stuff group of friends, Valerie hopes to complete her children's book about Edinburg's Vietnam Veteran Freddy Gonzalez. She was inspired to write it after seeing pictures of Freddy as a child in *When the River Dreams* by John W. Flores and by visiting with Freddy's mother Dolia.

Loving history has always been an important part of her life and Valerie has spent the last two decades plus serving on the Hidalgo County Historical Commission. Mrs. Ramírez has helped facilitate Edinburg's celebration of the Texas state holiday

Juneteenth or Emancipation Day. The year 2018 marked the twenty-fifth anniversary of the annual memorial observance at Restlawn, the African American section of Hillcrest Cemetery. She has also documented the history of African Americans in the Rio Grande Valley by donating materials to local archives and preparing outdoor informational signs in Edinburg at Restlawn and in McAllen at the former Bethel Missionary Baptist Church site on S. 16th Street. Valerie hopes her endeavors will assist in bringing about more unity and understanding among diverse groups of people.

Shrouding Margaret

(Washing and wrapping the body of a departed loved one is a burial practice in the Baha'i Faith of which Margaret was a member.)

1. The Women

First on the scene was a retired military nurse. She led the charge, accompanied by her dog (which stayed in the car) and a bag of required items: the burial ring, rose water, and towels.

Next came a former dentist, accustomed to blood and bones, and her child who was from the same stock. The rambunctious daughter had grown into a compassionate and capable woman. They brought me with them.

Then appeared the anxious newcomer, "Don't go," advised her long-distance-phone-call mother. "You'll faint. Let someone else do it." But there she stood, with a brave heart, ready to assist.

The final one to arrive was Margaret's tearful, dedicated soul sister, determined to fulfill one last act of service for her departed friend.

2. The Entrance

We gathered in the beautiful, well-lit funeral home lobby and chatted, happy to see one another. I was blissfully ignorant of what was to come. My only previous shrouding experience had taken place in my friend's comfortable nursing-home room.

The director's painted nails pressed numbers on the big silver door's key pad. As it opened, we stepped into a cold, sterile setting. Our group entered the first room and we walked past a covered body on a table to the left. I didn't turn my head to take a closer look. I knew it wasn't Margaret because our guide kept on walking to a second door.

Once we were all inside the second room, the funeral director began giving instructions and handing out little plastic bags with sterile gowns inside. As I passed mine on to the next lady, I prayed, "Dear God, please help me get through this."

Unfortunately, I noticed the needles in the stainless steel sink. When I turned away, I saw the table with another covered body. I knew this was my friend.

"Sterile gloves are a must," declared the professional and I thought, *Margaret's already gone. There's nothing that can hurt her now.* But I hurt. My stomach tightened and my ears rang as that funny feeling crept into them. "Remember, the door must stay closed and locked. I'll be right outside if you need anything."

"We're going to pray first," explained one of the women.

3. The Exit

"I'm going to pray outside," I interjected and left with the director. She guided me out the nearest exit and to a bench. The breeze stroked my face and the tears began. I prayed between sobs, rocking gently with my head in my hands.

"Ma'am do you want some water?" a gentleman asked. I nodded yes. He also brought a box of tissues. They were softer than the bathroom's paper towel I had saved in my pocket.

I continued my outside vigil, pausing to watch the fog lift and to listen to the birds sing. Every once in a while the man's gentle voice would come again saying, "Are you okay? Do you need anything?"

"No, thank you," I would whisper back, grateful for his attention.

After some time, maybe an hour, I heard familiar voices from inside and soon a friend appeared. "We're done. Do you want to come in?"

4. Gratitude

I nodded yes and re-entered the building. We walked back to the first room through the unlocked door. Margaret's simple wooden coffin was open and there she lay, wrapped in her white cotton shroud. Only her swollen face was exposed. No eyebrows were penciled in and each nostril held a cotton ball.

"There were some embalming leaks when we turned her body, explained the young, anxious one who didn't faint.

"How did you do it?" I asked.

"I went into my 'just suck it up and get through this' zone, she answered.

So young, so pretty, so tough, I thought. This is what escaping religious persecution of the Baha'is in Iran and being a refugee had engendered in her. I admired her and I respected them all, grateful that they had granted Margaret's final wish.

"Did you put the ring on her finger?" I questioned.

"Yes, she's wearing it," came the reply. The inscription reads: I came forth from God, and return unto Him.

I nodded and offered a final prayer. That was all I could contribute to Margaret's shrouding. The rest was left to the funeral home. There were no pall bearers, so her casket was taken unaccompanied to the nearby grave site for the afternoon service.

5. Farewell

And so, my dear friend, what my hands could not accomplish with cloth, they have attempted to achieve with words to lovingly wrap and send you on the way to your heavenly abode which tongue cannot tell, nor pen recount. May it be acceptable – Godspeed. Rest in peace.

Restlawn:
A Cemetery's Story Retold
for Juneteenth Emancipation
Day 2018

Restlawn – sacred ground
tell us of your saints and sinners.

Reveal the secrets of those who lived and died
in the days of segregation.

Mothers, fathers, sisters, brothers, and children.
Aunts and uncles. Friends and neighbors.
All are in attendance. Waiting and watching.
Hoping for a better day.

Crossing over that bridge to join with all of us.
Remember their names.
Remember their past.
It is ours as well.

But look at today – see the faces?
We are not all one color, but many.
Here together, celebrating Freedom.

The Hand of God

In recognition of the Creator of the heavens and the
earth and whatever lieth between them and in honor
of the August 2017 eclipse

It seemed to me as if the hand of God were moving
across the sky,
casting its shadow on the land
then ending in the sea.
It caught my attention.

For some brief moments,
the multiple contentions seen on the news
became very petty.
And the violent hatreds temporarily subsided.

Diverse people gathered together harmoniously
to watch and wait
for the flash of that diamond in the sky.

Feverish brows cooled and daylight turned to night
and then returned again.
Many bore witness that day to the power of God that
cannot be eclipsed.

The Mistress of Santa Cruz Gardens

For my master-gardener and naturalist friend
Sylvia Casselman

The mistress of Santa Cruz Gardens
is not a master of anything.
She holds no advanced degrees;
yet, she advances.

Day by day, month by month,
and year by year along her path of service,
until hopefully, at last,
she will arrive at her destination.

Sergeant Freddy Gonzalez

In honor of the 50th anniversary of his passing
February 4, 2018

Who was Freddy Gonzalez and what did he do to
make us remember him so?

He began as a child pretty much like you
who loved to play with his family and friends.

The years passed by and the boy grew into a strong,
young man – a Marine.
And as soldiers sometimes must, Freddy fought and
died in a land far away
sacrificing himself for the people and country he
loved.

Who could forget such a man?
Not his family or friends.
Not his country.
Not me and I hope not you.

Cemetery Saturday Night

For June 19 (Juneteenth), 1995

The air is cool and refreshing -
the night clear with crickets singing.

Stars shine down upon us
like headlights of 18-wheelers
flying by on the overpass above,
as they rush on into the darkness.

From the radio, Cab Calloway blares out into the
night.

It feels like a party and I wonder
where are you dancing as we move quietly
among the graves pouring water from gallon jugs
onto your memories.

Sunset came too quickly and the magic of darkness
caught our souls here together.

For one brief moment, as the music plays,
we celebrate as one on this Saturday night.

www.ingramcontent.com/pod-product-compliance
Lightning Source LLC
Chambersburg PA
CBHW031308170626
46807CB00001B/334